D1273222

VERNON J. BOURKE, Ph.D., was born in North Bay, Ontario, Canada in 1907. He did his undergraduate work at St. Michael's College in the University of Toronto. In 1937 he received his Doctorate in Philosophy from the Institute of Mediaeval Studies.

From 1928 to 1931 he was Lecturer in Greek Philosophy at the University of Toronto. Since 1931 Professor Bourke has been associated with the Department of Philosophy at St. Louis University. He was made full professor in 1946.

Doctor Bourke was made an Honorary Member of the Société Philosophique de Louvain (Belgium) in 1959. In 1963 he was awarded the Aquinas Medal of the American Catholic Philosophical Association. He has been a delegate of the American Catholic Philosophical Association to the International Congress of Philosophy on three separate occasions.

Articles by Professor Bourke have appeared in more than twenty-five philosphy journals in the United States, Europe and South America. He is the author of three books in the field of philosophy, and has contributed to four others either as translator or editor. He also serves as advisory editor to *Speculum, The Modern Schoolman* and *The Natural Law Forum.*

WILL IN
WESTERN THOUGHT

WILL IN
WESTERN THOUGHT

An Historico-Critical Survey
by VERNON J. BOURKE

SHEED AND WARD - NEW YORK

McCORMICK THEOLOGICAL SEMINARY
McGAW MEMORIAL LIBRARY
800 WEST BELDEN AVENUE
CHICAGO, ILLINOIS 60614

© *Sheed and Ward, Inc. 1964*

Library of Congress Catalog Card Number 64-13569

Manufactured in the United States of America

BF
611
B774w

Preface

THIS BOOK TOOK its origin in a long-standing personal conviction that the meaning of *will* in the history of Western
philosophy is not as simple and uniform as many writers take
it to be. In a graduate seminar in philosophy at St. Louis
University, during the academic year 1960–61, twenty-
seven students investigated various theories of volition from
the time of the Greeks to the present. Their studies frankly
amazed me and I should like to acknowledge their contribution to this book by giving their names: Father J. P. Assion,
Mr. W. M. Bichl, S.J., Mr. J. F. Britt, Father H. R. Burns,
S.J., Mr. M. J. Carella, Mr. D. J. Carville, S.J., Father T. P.
Casper, Mr. D. J. Collins, S.J., Mr. C. A. Corr, Mr. T. A.
Duggan, S.J., Sister Dorothy Ann Dunn, I.H.M., Sister
Thomas Marguerite Flanigan, C.S.J., Mr. J. A. Haas, Mr.
P. Heinbecker, Sister M. Angele Hotze, Mr. A. A. Keith,
Mr. G. J. Koob, S.J., Mr. J. Mace, S.J., Father P. McLaugh-
lin, Brother C. Patrick McMahon, F.S.C., Mr. R. Miller, S.J.,
Father E. W. Ranly, C.PP.S., Mr. B. Roy, S.J., Father J. T.
Schuett, S.J., the Rev. Mr. E. Stahlnecker, Mr. E. C. Toomey,
and Brother Cosmas G. Vreeland, F.S.C.

Needless to say, I have not been able to utilize all of the
material on philosophical and psychological theories of volition which was uncovered in this seminar. From this re-

search, however, I was enabled to pinpoint what seemed to be the most significant views, as a guide to my own reading. The presentation of this material is my own, as is the interpretation.

In 1962, Boston College celebrated its Centenary and invited me to give a series of twenty lectures on this subject during November of that year. This provided an opportunity to organize the thousands of pages of notes which I had assembled into a more compact and, it is hoped, understandable form. My special thanks are due to the Reverend Frederick J. Adelmann, S.J., Chairman of the Department of Philosophy at Boston College, and to the various officers of the administration of that University for their invitation and encouragement.

Finally, the editors of Sheed & Ward, Inc. indicated an interest in bringing out the lectures in book form. With some revision, what follows is the resultant. It only remains to express my gratitude to Mr. Philip Scharper, Mr. James P. Haughey, and their associates at Sheed & Ward, for their interest, their valuable suggestions for the revision, and for their assistance in seeing the book through the press.

VERNON J. BOURKE

Contents

Contents

WILL IN
WESTERN THOUGHT

CHAPTER I

What Does Will Mean?

WE PROPOSE TO STUDY the chief meanings that have been given to *will* in Occidental philosophy and then try to determine whether there is one univocal way of using will, a meaning that would seem most appropriate for contemporary philosophical work. There would be at least one other method of handling this problem: this would entail starting with a certain notion of what will means and then going through the history of philosophy in search of those who have given this preconceived meaning to will. It might even include criticisms of such a meaning. One could, for instance, begin with the view that will means "rational appetite" (as it does for Thomas Aquinas) and then investigate the various explanations of rational appetition that have been offered in the course of Western philosophical thought. With this method, it would not matter whether a given thinker used the language of will, provided he discussed the points included in the initial definition. This would be an interesting and profitable study but it is not what we are going to do. Such an investigation would exclude, by virtue of the initial definition, much interesting material on the subject.

In one sense, what we shall do is a word study, an essay in historical semantics. The English word, will, has cognates in most of the languages of the Western world. One has only to look briefly at an etymological dictionary to see that will is connected with a group of very similar words in the north European languages that have the root "wil" or "vil" with the variants "wol" or "vol." Thus the Anglo-Saxon noun is *willa*, the German *Wille*, the Danish *ville*. These forms resemble the Latin infinitive *velle* but are not derived from it. In Russian, the noun is *volya* (воля); in German the verb form is *wollen*; in English we have corresponding forms such as *volition* and *voluntary*. These resemble the Latin noun *voluntas*, from which are derived many of the south European forms: French *volonté*, Italian *volontà*, Spanish *voluntad*, and so on. Classical Greek has boulesis (βούλησις) which is pronounced *voulesis* in modern Greek, and verb forms in which the root "boul" is obviously related to the Latin "vol." Etymologists trace these forms back to a Sanskrit root "vri" and further to a basic Aryan root "WAR" (WAL) which, they say, meant "to choose, to like, to will."[1] It is fascinating (though not perhaps philosophically valuable) to investigate the variants in such a family of words. Irish Gaelic, for example, has the form "TOIL" in which the initial "T" becomes silent and the word sounds much like the English, will.[2] Arabic has *irâda* for will, a form which may be related to the Sanskrit root.[3] In short, the preceding is sufficient to indicate that most of the languages of Western philosophy, ancient, medieval and modern, have words that are morphologically related to our word, will.

Dictionary definitions of these "vol-wil-vri" words underline their similarity of basic meaning. This may be illustrated by reference to two commonly used English dictionaries. *Webster's Collegiate* defines will, first, in terms of a set of activities: wish, desire, inclination, pleasure, choice, intention. Later, it mentions "the power of choosing . . . and of acting in accordance with choice."[4] On the other hand, a typical small British dictionary opens its entry on will by saying that it is, "the faculty or power of mind by which we decide to do or not to do," and later it gives the meaning in terms of activities.[5] Of course, we do not expect technical philosophical explanations from general dictionaries, but we may note the American emphasis on the activity, or functional meaning, and the more traditional British stress on the faculty meaning.

Turning to one of the most recent philosophical dictionaries in English, we find two entries on will. One written by Ledger Wood starts off by saying: "Will: a) in the widest sense, will is synonymous with conation. See *Conation.*" Then it proceeds to analyze an act of willing into the envisaging of alternative courses of action, deliberation, and decision or choice. When one looks at conation, in this dictionary, one finds Vergilius Ferm neatly completing the circle by saying: "Referring to voluntary activity."[6] There is a second entry by Rudolf Allers which gives the Scholastic meaning of will as, "one of the two rational faculties of the human soul." A more formal Scholastic definition is offered in Wuellner's *Dictionary*: "the rational appetite; that power of the human soul or of a spiritual substance which tends toward a good apprehended by the intellect, or away from an evil recognized by the intellect." He adds that will also designates any act of this appetite.[7] A comparable French dictionary of philosophy lists will (*volonté*) as the faculty of activity.[8] Perhaps these examples are sufficient to suggest that we cannot learn what will really means by consulting philosophical dictionaries, either.

Nor is much precise information to be found in the usual histories of philosophy. As a rule, such works treat the views on logic, theory of knowledge, reality and ethics of the thinkers in a given period, or in the whole of Western philosophy. Speculation on the problems of volition is only occasionally treated and that in cases (such as Schopenhauer) where will is extremely basic to a man's thought. Much the same is true of histories of psychology. There are some psychological monographs on the activities of willing but these are restricted to very limited problems and techniques of observation and usually presuppose some philosophical meaning of will.[9]

It would be valuable to study the use of will-language in the great classics of Western literature: in the Greek dramatists, in the Roman essayists and poets, in medieval poetry (secular and religious), in Dante, Shakespeare and the Russian novelists. Obviously, this would be a lengthy task. It will not be undertaken here. Instead, we shall limit our field to the views of will that can be found in the philosophical literature of the ancient, medieval and modern periods. Philosophy is here taken in a broad sense, so as not to exclude theology in centuries when these disciplines were closely associated. Nor shall we ignore modern psychological writings.

One way of making this investigation would be to write a history of philosophy, taking will and volition as a central interest and treating the various thinkers in schools or in chronological order. I must confess that this is what I had in mind originally. However, such a detailed and necessarily repetitive history of will theories does not now appear to be the best instrument for understanding what will has meant to Western philosophers. In effect, I have assembled such a chronological account, in preliminary research notes, and it is a welter of materials which requires further organization.[10]

A survey of this collection of notions on will suggests that Western thinkers have taken eight distinctive views of the subject. These divisions are not exhaustive, nor are they entirely exclusive of each other, but they are sufficiently characteristic of different ways of looking at will.

Will Means Intellectual Preference

Philosophers in a first group either identify, or associate very closely, the notion of willing with the act of *intellectual judgment*. These are people who tend to be classified as "intellectualists" in histories of ethics. Broadly speaking, when they talk about will or volition, they mean an act of *intelligent preference*. Obviously, they are the kind of men who say that virtue is practical knowledge. To thinkers of a different temperament or persuasion, these intellectualists appear to have sacrificed will to the all-consuming maw of cognition. Yet they do use the language of volition and at times offer quite thorough explanations of activities such as intending, choosing and enjoying.

Chapter Two will attempt to show that this association of willing with intellectual or rational preference is characteristic of Greek philosophy up to and including Aristotle. It is, indeed, one important aspect of the Greek cult of reason. Moreover, we shall observe that some medieval thinkers understand will in this way. In modern philosophy, thinkers as dissimilar on other matters as Spinoza and Hobbes share something of this intellectualist approach to will. We shall even see that Kant, in one of his ways of understanding will, is an intellectualist.

Will Means Rational Appetite

A second way of looking at will is to regard it as a special kind of *appetite*. In this sense, appetite means a power or tendency to incline toward objects that are apprehended as good and away from objects that are known as not good. Appetite is taken, usually, as a power or faculty of a generic character which may be subdivided into several species.

Thinkers in this second group sometimes sharply distinguish sensory appetition from rational appetition. Thus psychic appetites may be either: (1) *sensory* (which incline toward or away from individual objects known through sense perception) or (2) *intellectual* (whose functions are inclinations toward or away from universal objects apprehended through intellect or reason). The latter, intellectual appetite, is also called will.

In the case of the Stoics, however, we have a rational appetite theory of will that does not entail a sharp differentiation of will from sensory appetition. It is in Plotinus, John Damascene, Albert the Great and Thomas Aquinas that will comes to be more and more identified with intellectual appetite and progressively more distinguished from sensory inclination.

The use of appetite as a *genus*, of which will is one species, means that this second group of thinkers do not necessarily associate freedom with all activities of willing. In point of fact, Thomas Aquinas describes some volitional inclinations that are not free and others that are. In expositions of such a theory, it is rare to find the term "free will." Freedom is attributed to actions such as choice or decision, and these are understood to be volitional acts. Personally free actions are not interpreted as simple acts of will but become complex functions of two powers, intellect and will. Yet these thinkers who identify will with rational appetite are not "intellectualists" in the sense that the group-one thinkers are. Men like Thomas Aquinas do not say that willing is essentially an act of intellect; they make a radical distinction between cognition and appetition. In Thomism, willing is never identified with pure cognition. However, certain human activities, such as choosing, are not taken as exclusive functions of will. This notion is to be treated more fully in Chapter Three. Please do not misunderstand this point: what has here been said briefly, and will be shown more fully later, concerning the view of Thomas Aquinas is not to be understood as applicable to so-called neo-Thomists or to all later Scholastic thinkers. Very few modern "Thomists" offer an explanation of willing that is recognizable as that of Aquinas. Modern Scholasticism has adopted a view of volition that incorporates factors from Scotism, Suarezianism, Cartesianism and even from British Associationism.

Freedom as the Genus of Volition

We find a third school of philosophers who take *freedom* as the essential characteristic of will and volition. These are the men who practically never speak of will without saying free will. To them, will means radical spontaneity of action or decision. Sometimes it means uncaused and completely unconditioned activity. Will is another way of saying liberty. Holders of this view usually engage in endless controversies with "determinists"—and they regard those who take our first two views of will as determinists.

Sometimes this third position is called "voluntarism," because it is often associated with the claim that willing is a more important activity than knowing. This assertion of the primacy of will may be found in reference to the divine will, to the human will, or to both. In Chapter Four, we shall illustrate this view, that will is liberty, by an examination of the positions of Duns Scotus, William of Ockham and other fourteenth-century writers. Modern philosophy offers Descartes as the most prominent and influential exponent of the idea that will is freedom. The famous theory of "liberty of indifference" becomes an important tangent of this third approach to will. Later, the identification of will with freedom is seen in German idealism; it is especially prominent in the thought of Fichte and Schopenhauer. Many recent Catholic writers also support the view that the human will is essentially free in all its activities.

Will Means Dynamic Power

A fourth usage in regard to will seems to identify it with energy, or *motor power*. If the third group approaches willing in terms of final causality, this fourth school may be said to view volition as an aspect of efficient causality. There is some evidence of such a shift in later medieval philosophy but the fourth meaning becomes quite evident in modern British philosophy. David Hume, for instance, regards will as a psychological impression of *effort*, occurring whenever a person produces a bodily or mental movement.[11] With the further development of Associationism, we find Alexander Bain plainly identifying will with spontaneity of movement in the human body. To will is to do something with the feeling that a person is directing his own movements. Of course, this view has continued to hold a prominent place in later English, French and American thought.

This same, or a very similar, notion (that will is personal or even biological energy) is advanced by thinkers who differ greatly on other philosophical questions. In a spiritualized context, it can be recognized in French thinkers, such as Maine de Biran and Victor Cousin. In quite another sense, it is characteristic of Schopenhauer and Nietzsche: they do not say that will is illustrated at its best in bodily activity but, fundamentally for them, corporeal motion (as a sort of epiphenomenon) is a low-grade manifestation of *Wille*.

However, the neatest presentation of this fourth theory is offered in the literature of faculty psychology in the United

States.[12] This nineteenth-century school strongly maintained that each man has three specifically human "faculties." For readers familiar with Scholasticism, it is important to note that there is little resemblance between this kind of faculty psychology and medieval theories of the powers of man's soul. The American psychologists of the last century claimed that man is endowed with the faculties of *understanding*, *heart* (also called sensibility or taste), and *will*. In this analysis, will becomes a kind of executive capacity. Guided by the faculty of heart, the will carries out the desires or affections of the human agent. Understanding is the knowing power; heart or sensibility is the feeling power; and will is the acting or efficient power.

We shall examine this interesting way of understanding will, as dynamic power, in Chapter Five.

Heart, Affection and Will

There is, historically, a fifth set of thinkers who concentrate on will as the *seat of love*, or as *love itself*. Of course, nearly all philosophies of will regard love as a very distinctive volitional function. Yet there is a special way of looking at divine and human willing, a view that is usually expressed in what may be called the "heart-language." We shall see how prominent this usage is in the Bible and in Hebrew thought. The *heart* is taken as the seat of the highest spiritual affections, of the most intimate knowledge and decisions. In some medieval Jewish writers, the heart becomes the whole soul. Saadia ben Joseph (in the early tenth century) can be considered as a prime example of this view.

Obviously, many Christian writers also speak of man's heart as exercising certain functions, or feeling certain affections, which are in other places attributed to will by the same authors. Augustine of Hippo is an excellent example but this use of "heart" is a common feature of Christian spiritual literature. The heart-language is even applied to the divine will, in the well-known devotion to the Sacred Heart and in many similar contexts.

What is not so well known is that this use of the heart-language to designate volitional activities (such as loving, deciding, commanding) has a medical origin in Greek times.[13] We shall examine this development in one school of Greek medicine, that of Diokles of Karystos in the third century B.C. Various later schools of Greek psychology held the notion that there is a sort of governing principle (the *hegemonikon*) in each man which is the center of human personality. It is a sort of ruling will, often located in the heart as a physical organ. Sometimes this principle is called the *pneuma* (spirit) which is taken in either a subtle corporeal sense (breath) or in a quasi-immaterial sense.

Clearly, the use of the heart-language as expressive of volitional functions has continued, especially in poetry and works of piety. In cruder symbolization it has been commercialized by the makers of valentines. This usage is so widespread and accepted in many languages and literatures that we might say that "heart" is not merely a symbol of love and spiritual affection but even that heart has now two quite distinct meanings: (1) a blood pump in the biological organism; (2) the seat of love and other activities of willing. Of course, most thinkers who use the heart-language (and this includes some of the least romantic writers in the history of philosophy) also equate heart with will. That is why the usage will be discussed in our sixth chapter. On this point, American faculty psychology is a major exception, for this school radically distinguishes heart from will.

The Will of the People

A sixth view of will understands volition as a *group* phenomenon: this is the famous theory of the "will of the people." The very concept of a political "election" suggests that a group of men is capable of making a collective choice which expresses, or is, the will of the collectivity. Perhaps this is one of the cornerstones of democratic practice but we shall note (in Chapter Seven) how theories of group will can be easily turned to support other extremes of political philosophy. At times, it has not been difficult to persuade the "people" that one man personifies their joint will, or that a certain class of men is the epitome of the will of the whole people. What should be determined here is whether this notion of a collective will can be, or has been, developed into a philosophically distinctive meaning of volition. Heretofore, we have been dealing with views of willing that are personal; now, in this sixth usage, will is made to transcend the person.

The concept of a will of the people is not prominent in ancient or medieval thought, though there are approaches to it in the later middle ages.[14] Marsilius of Padua, in the fourteenth century, makes a start on this theory of volition. In modern philosophy, it is with Jean Jacques Rousseau that this view of will reaches full development. His idea of a general will has become one of the bases of the contract theory of political organization. The psychology of group volition is basic to Rousseau's social contract.[15] Edmund Burke's violent reaction to this concept in Rousseau shows how important the theory of the will of the people had become in eighteenth-century political philosophy. Of course, John Locke brought the theory of the will of the majority to a dominant position in British political thought at the end of the seventeenth century. Precisely what such a group will meant

to Locke is not easy to determine; it certainly did not mean
that the state is a natural organism with a natural power of
willing. Locke equates will with certain activities. His will of
the people, we shall see, consists in actions of decision and
choice performed by citizens. Though he is commonly regarded as a great libertarian, the philosopher of political
freedom, Locke is quite unconcerned about the freedom of
certain minorities in the body politic. He advocated the suppression of Catholicism, for instance, in England. In any case,
Locke's notion of the public will exerted an important influence on the men who planned the United States of America.

In modern German idealism, the "will of the people" notion followed a different tangent. In the political writings of
Fichte, at the end of the eighteenth century, we already
encounter the view that will is something greater than the
individual man. In one sense, for Fichte the infinite and
eternal "Will" is God. In another sense, will as common and
generic is embodied in the state and is a supra-human energy
or impetus which transcends the mere wishes of individuals.
Here we are in the midst of a kind of political voluntarism
that is easily turned into a mystique of the manifest destiny of
a certain "people." This continues in Hegel's speculations on
the inevitable unfolding of universal will in history. In perverted form, the transcendent will of the German *Volk* was
used by Alfred Rosenberg and other prophets of National Socialism to lend philosophical respectability to totalitarianism.[16]

Varied uses of the will of the people continue in contemporary political and social thought. It is still commonly accepted that a public figure bows to the will of the people
when he accepts nomination or election to office, and that a
political executive or legislator carries out the will of the people in his official functions. Precisely what this public will

means, and by what means it is determined, are points of some obscurity.[17]

Will as the Source of Law

Many thinkers have regarded will (divine, human, or both) as *that which originates law*. Perhaps this concept of the legislative will occasions no present surprise, for we live in a period in which legal voluntarism is a widely accepted point of view. This has not always been the case. A good many people in the ancient and medieval periods thought that reason is the source of law and that will has no essential part in its origination. Thomas Aquinas is typical; his famous definition of law as, "an ordinance of reason promulgated for the common good by someone in charge of the community,"[18] represents a non-voluntaristic view of law. On the other hand, there is another medieval tradition running through the thirteenth and fourteenth centuries which stresses the need of an act of will, on the part of the legislator, before a law can be validly constituted.[19] Quite possibly, this way of looking at will as legislative could be traced back to much earlier seeds in Christian tradition. After all, one petition in the Lord's Prayer reads: "Thy will be done on earth, as it is in heaven."[20] Throughout the Old Testament the Will of God is respected, and at times feared, as the source of order and regulation in human life. It is not surprising, then, that many later medieval thinkers take the divine will as the supreme fount of law and the will of the human law-maker as the source of man-made laws. This view is very clearly developed by William of Ockham.

The early *Essays* of John Locke (recently edited) offer an important modern instance of the attribution of a law-making function to will, both human and divine. William Paley is another British advocate of the legislative divine will. However, the concept of will as legislative is most distinctive of the thought of Immanuel Kant. We shall take him as the typical representative of this position. Kant's way of using will is complicated by a duality of terms (*Wille* and *Willkür*) with different connotations. We shall study the sense in which *Wille*, as practical reason, elicits law.

Both British and American legal philosophies of the present century have been much influenced by legal positivism. This is simply the theory that the sovereign will is the law. We are not so much interested, in this study, in what this does with law as in the sort of will that the position implies. Such a will is not only primary and unconditioned; it appears to exercise certain cognitive functions. The legislative will seems to know what should be done and what should be forbidden. A typical British instance of the legislative will is found in the jurisprudence of John Austin, where will and law are practically identified.[21] It is odd that such legal voluntarism has taken hold in American judicial and legislative thinking, for it makes it very difficult to maintain the traditional distinction of the three branches of government, legislative, judicial and executive. Voluntaristic positivism seems to require the supremacy of the legislature and the consequent reduction of the judiciary and the executive to the role of agents of the legislator. It is not possible to have three distinct but equally sovereign wills. We shall return to this point.

Will and Reality

A final way in which philosophers have used will identifies it with *basic reality*. This develops into a sort of metaphysics of volition. Such a usage of the term, will, is not uncommon in Western philosophy but it is so far removed from the speech of the ordinary non-philosopher that this meaning goes unrecognized in standard dictionaries. The fact of the matter is that several key philosophers have insisted that *to be* is *to will*.

As a first example of this view, we shall consider Plotinus' theory of volition. Unlike the pre-Christian Greeks who (with the exception of the Stoics) have little to say about will, Plotinus is a Greek philosopher, in the Christian era though not himself a Christian, who made quite a study of volitional activity. For him, reality is dynamic in character: a being is what it does. Since Plotinus also thought that the ultimate source of existing reality is immaterial, rather obviously his account of the emanation of the many from the One will be couched in terms of either the process of cognition or that of volition. It can be shown that Plotinus uses both processes. Indeed, his notion of real energy may be fundamentally voluntaristic. To say that Plotinus discusses the descent of the many from the One, in terms of willing (*boulesis*), does not at all mean that he sees this process as a free one. The emanation of a multiplicity of things is a necessary development. Hence, Plotinus tries to describe the inevitable tendency of the One to diffuse itself as a necessary desire of the good.[22] In other words, Plotinus' use of will language is an important instance of the appetite theory. However, he adds to this the suggestion that reality itself is appetitive, energetic, of the nature of willing.

Medieval philosophy is not without similar views. There was a great deal of Jewish speculation in the middle ages concerning the Will of God, both as to whether it might properly be termed free and also as to whether it was identical with God or more like a first creature of God. One solution to this problem is offered by the twelfth-century Jewish thinker, Avicebron (Ibn Gabirol), who decided that the divine will, when not acting, is identical with God's essence—but when acting, the Will of God becomes an intermediary between the divine essence and the things of this universe.[23] The reason for such a complicated problem and answer is that the Jewish thinkers knew the Old Testament suggestion that the Will of God changes—and they did not care to attribute change to God Himself. In any case, Avicebron, while not a typical Jewish teacher, is a good example of a man who takes divine will as the immediate principle or even constituent of reality, although he does not make the divine will to be materially identical with the whole universe.

Much the same problem, and consequent efforts to relate divine will with created realities, are discoverable in the writings of some medieval Mohammedan theologians. The tenth-century school of Al Ash'ari, for instance, regarded the world as having a sort of phenomenal existence in space and time, and thought of the will of Allah as a bond which holds the parts of reality in existence. Without this binding force, the whole structure would collapse into nothing.[24] Of course, Christians also believe that God must support the world of creation in every moment of its existence and action. However, Christian theologians do not usually regard the divine will as part of the fabric of creation.

In point of fact, we do find some seventeenth-century Christian philosophers who practically deny that men and the things of this world have any reality outside the will of God. This view either makes divine will identical with reality or it denies reality to finite existents. Nicholas Malebranche is a Catholic example of such a thinker; Arnold Geulincx is a Protestant contemporary with very similar teachings. In the case of Malebranche, a creature is nothing but "an act of volition which persists and operates without ceasing."[25] This volition is an act of divine will which constitutes whatever limited reality may be granted to the end-product of creation.

The best example of a philosopher who has identified will with reality is Schopenhauer. His metaphysical voluntarism is but one instance of a continuing movement in nineteenth-century German idealism. We shall see why Schelling has been described as maintaining that "reality is, through and through, action, life, will."[26] Fichte, in turn, suggests that will is a primitive force in both the visible and the invisible worlds. There is here no question of will meaning simply a series of human actions, or a power of the human spirit: instead, will now becomes the very stuff of reality. There are passages in Hegel where will is presented as the material in which the dialectical process takes place.[27] But it remained for Schopenhauer to create a full-blown metaphysics of will.

Actually, Schopenhauer made a rather thorough investigation of various treatments of will in the history of philosophy. He found a text in Clement of Alexandria, for instance, where this Greek Father of the Church said that, "to will takes precedence over all other actions."[28] Schopenhauer resurrected the problem of Buridan's Ass, an animal supposedly situated between two equally luscious piles of hay and unable to make a choice. We now know that this ass is nowhere to be found in the extant writings of John Buridan and Schopenhauer was able to show that some elements of the story go back to Aristotle.[29] Most of the positions of the classical modern philosophers who have treated will are reviewed by Schopenhauer and he rejects the notion that man's will is free with a liberty of indifference. Eventually, he argues for a transcendent freedom of willing. The most striking conclusion that he comes to, however, is that all reality is will. In Kantian terms, will is the thing-in-itself.[30]

Of course, will is identified with the real in several other

types of recent European philosophy, notably in the writings
of Maine de Biran, Charles Secrétan and less clearly in the
thought of Henri Bergson. Most interesting to the American
reader is the prominent role played by a metaphysics of will,
in the philosophy of Josiah Royce. One usually thinks of his
absolute idealism as a type of intellectualism in which logic is
dominant but Royce has written:

I have myself long since maintained that there is indeed a logic
of the will, just as truly as there is a logic of the intellect. Personally, I go further still. I assert: all logic is the logic of the
will.[31]

We shall examine these main instances of metaphysical
voluntarism in our ninth chapter.

At the end of this introductory chapter, it should be admitted that there are inherent difficulties in making such a
quick survey of volitional theories. Obviously, each major
philosopher has his own complete philosophical view, his
Weltanschauung. What he says about will or volition should
be understood in function of his whole philosophy. Yet it is
impossible for me to offer even an adequate summary of these
many types of philosophy. To attempt this would be to
present a complete history of philosophy. All that one can do
in this regard is to warn the reader that the study of these
various will theories presupposes some acquaintance with the
basic philosophies of these thinkers whose volitional theories
are to be examined.

For the ancient philosophers some general work, such as
Zeller's *Outlines*,[32] would be a satisfactory thing to read. For
the medieval period, one could recommend Gilson's *History*.[33] Finally, a very reliable survey of modern philosophy is

to be found in the book by James Collins.[34] These histories of philosophy provide something of the background prerequisite to the special study on which we are embarking.

In Chapter Ten an attempt is made to offer what is called a core-meaning for the term will. It is clear that some men in the history of philosophy have over-extended the meaning of the word. We shall try to see what is central and philosophically useful, today, in the notion of volition. The resultant core-meaning is not presented as normative but simply as an effort at unifying an admittedly diffuse and variegated mass of meanings.

NOTES

1. See W. W. Skeat, *An Etymological Dictionary of the English Language* (Oxford: Clarendon Press, 1888), pp. 711–742; Eric Partridge, *Origins. A Short Etymological Dictionary* (New York: Macmillan, 1959), p. 788 (at the word, *volition*).

2. Ulick J. Bourke, *The Aryan Origin of the Gaelic Race and Language* (London: Longmans, 1876), p. 258 (for TOIL in the Lord's Prayer in Erse or Irish Gaelic) and p. 262 (for the genitive TOLA in line 7 of the *Iliad*).

3. Georges Vajda, "Quelques publications russes," *Revue des études juives*, 98 (1934), 103; A. M. Goichon, *Lexique de la langue philosophique d'Ibn Sīnā* (Paris: Desclée de Brouwer, 1938), pp. 115, n. 234; 145, n. 282.

4. *Webster's New Collegiate Dictionary* (Springfield, Mass.: Merriam Co., 1953), p. 979.

5. *The Standard Imperial Dictionary of the English Language*, ed. Cecil Weatherly (Toronto: Musson Book Co.), 1925, p. 961.

6. *The Dictionary of Philosophy* (ed. D. D. Runes, New York: Philosophical Library, 1942), pp. 61 and 336.

7. B. Wuellner, *Dictionary of Scholastic Philosophy* (Milwaukee: Bruce, 1956), p. 135.

8. André Lalande, *Vocabulaire technique et critique de la philosophie* (4me éd., Paris: Société Française de Philosophie, 1938), vol. I,

237: "Faculté, pouvoir ou liberté de faire quelque chose. Spéciale-
ment: on appelle facultés de l'âme, l'intelligence, l'activité (ou comme
l'on disait autrefois, la volonté) et enfin la sensibilité."

9. Probably the most complete general survey was published at
the end of the nineteenth century: Archibald Alexander, *Theories of
the Will in the History of Philosophy* (New York: Scribner, 1898),
pp. IX-357.

10. Mortimer Adler's *The Idea of Freedom*, 2 vols. (New York:
Doubleday, 1958–1961), is an example of a parallel investigation. One
can admire the thoroughness with which Adler has directed this joint
study; yet the very size of the work makes it difficult to remember
what has been treated in its more than 1600 pages.

11. *A Treatise of Human Nature*, ed. Selby-Bigge (Oxford: Clarendon Press, 1888), p. 399.

12. For a quick sketch of this school: H. W. Schneider, *A History
of American Philosophy* (New York: Columbia University Press,
1946), pp. 232–237.

13. The point has been studied by Gérard Verbeke, *L'Evolution
de la doctrine du Pneuma* (Paris: Desclée de Brouwer, 1945), pp.
13–15.

14. Cf. Ewart Lewis, *Medieval Political Ideas* (London-New York:
Macmillan, 1954), I, 159–162; see also Thomas Aquinas, *On Kingship*, trans. Phelan-Eschmann (Toronto: Pontifical Institute of Mediaeval Studies, 1949), c. X (80), p. 46.

15. See John W. Chapman, *Rousseau—Totalitarian or Liberal?*
(New York: Columbia University Press, 1956).

16. Cf. V. J. Bourke, "The Philosophical Antecedents of German
National Socialism," *Thought*, XIV, 53 (1939), 225–242.

17. See the comments of Joseph Tussman in his *Obligation and the
Body Politic* (New York: Oxford University Press, 1960), pp. 97–98,
111–112.

18. St. Thomas Aquinas *Summa Theologiae*, I-II, 90, 4, c.

19. Cf. T. E. Davitt, *The Nature of Law* (St. Louis: Herder, 1951);
F. Oakley, "Medieval Theories of Law: William of Ockham and the
Significance of the Voluntarist Tradition," *Natural Law Forum*, 6
(1961), 65–83.

20. Matt. 6:10; Luke 11:2–4 omits this petition in the usual English
Catholic versions (*The Holy Bible*, New York: Douay Bible House,
1941, New Testament, p. 72; *The New Testament*, Paterson, N.J.:
St. Anthony Guild Press, 1941, p. 191). However, the Greek text in
St. Luke's Gospel, ed. John T. White (London: Longmans, Green,
1909), p. 55, does this give full petition: γενηθήτω τὸ θέλημά σου ὡς ἐν

οὐρανῷ καὶ ἐπι τῆς γῆς. (It is to be noted that this petition uses *thelema,* not *boulesis,* for will. Latin and many other Western languages use the *vol-wil* terms in this petition.)

21. Cf. F. C. S. Northrop, "Philosophical Issues in Contemporary Law," *Natural Law Forum,* 2 (1957), 48–52.

22. This is explained in *Enneades,* VI, 8, ed. E. Bréhier (Paris: Les Belles Lettres, 1938), tome VI, 2me partie, pp. 132–161.

23. J. Guttmann, *Die Philosophie des Salomon ibn Gabirol* (Göttingen 1889), pp. 265–266.

24. See L. Gardet et M.-M. Anawati, *Introduction à la théologie musulmane* (Paris: Vrin, 1948), pp. 52–66.

25. *Dialogues on Metaphysics and on Religion,* trans. M. Ginsberg (London: Allen and Unwin, 1925), p. 190.

26. Frank Thilly, *History of Philosophy* (New York: Holt, 1931), p. 451.

27. *Philosophy of History,* trans. J. Sibree (New York: Willey, 1900), p. 38.

28. A. Schopenhauer, *Parerga und Paralipomena* (*Sämtliche Werke,* A. Hübscher, Wiesbaden: Brockhaus, 1946), Bd. V, 143; citing Clement of Alexandria, *Stromata,* II, c. 17.

29. *Preisschrift über die Freiheit des Willens* (*Werke,* ed. cit., 1950), Bd. IV, pp. 58–59. On Buridan, see: E. J. Monahan, "Human Liberty and Free Will according to John Buridan," *Mediaeval Studies,* XVI (1954), 72–86.

30. See K. Kolenda's *Introduction* to Schopenhauer, *Essay on the Freedom of the Will* (New York: Liberal Arts Press, 1960), pp. vii–xii.

31. Josiah Royce, *William James and Other Essays* (New York: Macmillan, 1911): Essay IV: *The Problem of Truth,* p. 234.

32. E. Zeller, *Outlines of the History of Greek Philosophy,* revised by W. Nestle, trans. by L. R. Palmer, 13th ed. (New York: Meridian Books, 1955).

33. E. Gilson, *History of Christian Philosophy in the Middle Ages* (New York: Random House, 1955).

34. James Collins, *A History of Modern European Philosophy* (Milwaukee: Bruce, 1954).

Intellectual Preference and Will

A SIMPLE (but very inadequate) way of looking at will equates volition with intellectual preference. In this view, willing is basically a cognitive function of judging that one object of consideration is to be set above others. This is a statement of the pure position which is rarely found, in this simple form, in the history of philosophy. In the case of moral philosophies, the theory usually accompanies the teaching that virtue is knowledge and can be readily taught. The making of a personal decision is reduced to the problem of understanding the greater good. While we shall see approaches to this position in all periods of Western thought, the best example of this intellectualist theory of volition is doubtless found in the philosophy of Spinoza.

The classical Greek philosophers are, on the whole, intellectualists. From the reports in Xenophon and the early dialogues of Plato, it appears that Socrates held that the acquisition of practical wisdom brought with it the ability to choose and to act well. That virtue is knowledge is one of the best known Socratic teachings. Plato's *Protagoras*, for instance, begins with Socrates arguing that practical wisdom cannot be taught and the Sophist maintaining that it can. At the end of the dialogue, the positions are reversed and Socrates is suggesting that justice, temperance and courage are teachable types of knowledge.[1] In the *Nicomachean Ethics* the Socratic position is put very bluntly: "For Socrates was entirely opposed to the view in question, holding that there is no such thing as incontinence; no one, he said, when he judges acts against what he judges best—people act so only by reason of ignorance."[2] If these reports are correct, then Socrates did interpret willing as a cognitive function of judging.

Plato divides the psychic activities of man into three main types: the functions of the rational part (*logos*), of the spirited part (*thumos*), and of the appetitive part (*epithumia*).[3] Acts of willing are attributed to "reason." In the person whose reason is dominated by the two lower parts, volition does not occur. It is thus that tyrants are pictured in the *Gorgias:* their souls are taken over by the desire for power and consequently, "they do nothing which they will" (a boulontai).[4] The "Tale of Er" describes souls after death as choosing the sort of life that they are next to live.[5] Those who make a wise choice are the men who have learned to use their reason well, to understand what their experience of a previous life has taught them.[6] Plato recognizes acts of desire, below the level of reason, but when he speaks of *boulesis* he attributes it to *logos*.

Many interpreters of Aristotle profess to find in him a theory of "will" considered as a special power of the human soul. This is true of readers who have been influenced by Christian, Thomistic, or Scholastic traditions. Brennan, for instance, clearly attributes a "power of volition" to Aristotle.[7] Ross says: "It has often been complained that the psychology of Plato and Aristotle has no distinct conception of the will. Aristotle's doctrine of choice is clearly an attempt to formulate such a conception."[8] Let us reserve judgment, for the moment, and look at the texts.

Aristotle's *De Anima* reviews the psychologies of his predecessors and then offers a very thorough analysis and description of vegetative, sensory and intellectual functions. By the end of the Second Book, he has treated of many powers of sensory cognition (external and internal) and of a general power of desire(*orexis*) which is stimulated by sense presentations, and which (in its turn) stimulates the kinetic power of bodily movement. The discussion of imagination and internal sensing continues into the Third Book and leads into a theory of understanding (*nous*) which has occasioned much debate among Aristotelian commentators.[9] Apart from understanding, no other rational power is attributed, in Book III, to the human soul. There is some discussion of functions of desire (*orexis*) on the level of intelligence or reason, in the ninth and tenth chapters. Now, the point on which Aristotle insists is that there is but *one power* of desire or appetition (*orexis*) in one soul. He speaks, here, of wishing or willing (*boulesis*) but strongly maintains that it is a function of the one power in which all appetitive functions (sensory and intellectual) occur. After listing the first three general "parts" of the soul (nutritive, sensitive and imaginative), he names a fourth part:

the appetitive, which would seem to be distinct both in definition and in power from all hitherto enumerated.

It is absurd to break up the last-mentioned faculty, as these thinkers do [he is referring to some current theory, now unidentifiable, that there are plural "appetites" in the soul], for wish (*boulesis*) is found in the calculative part and desire and passion in the irrational; and if the soul is tripartite appetite will be found in all three parts.[10]

Lest this be misunderstood, as implying that there is a special power of "intellectual appetite," Aristotle repeats, in the next chapter, "that which moves therefore is a single faculty and the faculty of appetite."[11] He adds, again, that wish is a form of appetite.[12]

From this treatment, in the treatise *De Anima* or *On the Soul*, our conclusion is obvious: Aristotle is opposing psychologies which pluralize the appetitive powers of man by saying that there is one orectic faculty which functions on both the sensory and rational levels. This is the interpretation that is offered by later Greek and Arabian commentators. Thomas Aquinas, however, interprets this passage as teaching that there are three appetites (and so, three different powers of appetition) in the human soul![13]

The only other place in which Aristotle deals with this question is at the beginning of the Third Book of the *Nicomachean Ethics*. This is where he introduces his famous theory of self-controlled activity (*to hekousion*) and uncontrolled activity (*to akousion*). It is to be noted that the Greek names have no linguistic connection with the language of volition. Unfortunately, Latin and many modern languages translate *hekousion* as *voluntarium* (voluntary), thereby suggesting that we have, here, a full-blown theory of volition or will.[14]

Eventually, Aristotle does relate self-controlled activity to volitional functions but his initial discussion is conducted in terms of *knowledge* of what one is doing and of the purpose to which it is directed, and in terms of a certain spontaneity of personal activity. Choice (*proairesis*) is a selection of what is possible of attainment by one's own action; and choice is an instance of self-controlled activity (*hekousion*). Wishing (or willing, in a broad sense) is called *boulesis*; it is a willing of an end, irrespective of whether it is possible to attain it and of whether it is an end for oneself or for another person.[15] Deliberation (*boule*) is a cognitive consideration of several possible means to an end; it terminates in a judgment that one means is best. One chooses by desiring this means.

This analysis does not require Aristotle to postulate a separate faculty of "will" but it does indicate that he has moved beyond the pure position of will as intellectual preference. A practical cognitive judgment is essential to an act of choosing; yet there is some orectic (or desiderative) aspect to choice. Aristotle finds it difficult to say whether the central character of choice is a cognitive or an appetitive function. Later in the *Nicomachean Ethics*, he refuses to decide this point, saying: "choice is either desiderative reason or ratiocinative desire."[16] Perhaps the traditional Greek respect for reason was too strong in Aristotle to permit him to place the critical act of choice wholly in the area of desire. His theory of volition is partly an intellectual preference view but it is not fully developed.

In spite of the fact that the Stoics talked much about fate, and hence they are often classed as "determinists," this post-Aristotelian school discussed the nature of *boulesis* and tended to grant a certain psychological freedom to man's volitional functions. Zeno of Cittium distinguished eight parts or powers of the human soul: the cognitive power (*to dianoetikon*), speech, the procreative capacity, plus the five external senses.[17] One function of the cognitive power is to serve as the center of organic and psychic life, and thus to direct or govern all life activities. In this sense, the *dianoetikon* is also called the *hegemonikon*. Whatever volitional activities are recognized by the early Stoics, these are centered in the *hegemonikon*. It is chiefly a rational capacity and the early Stoic views on willing are close to the theory of intellectual preference. Cicero explains their position as follows:

Wherefore, as soon as anything that has the appearance of good presents itself, nature incites us to endeavor to obtain it. Now, where this strong desire is consistent and founded on prudence, it is by the Stoics called *boulesis*, and the name which we give it is volition; and this they allow to none but their wise man, and define it thus: Volition is a reasonable desire.[18]

Themistius wrote one of the most influential commentaries on Aristotle's *De Anima*, in the fourth century of the Christian era, but this Greek commentator adds nothing to the theory of will as rational desire. When Themistius' *Commentary* is translated into Latin, by William of Moerbeke in the thirteenth century, *boulesis* is called *voluntas* and Christian readers, such as Thomas Aquinas, interpret this function of wishing in the strong sense of an intellectually appetitive faculty.[19] Mohammedan interpreters of the *De Anima* (Avicenna and Averroes, eleventh and twelfth centuries) are faithful to the teaching of the original text and do not go beyond Aristotle's notions of general desire and intellectual preference.

St. Thomas Aquinas' theory of human willing is not an example of an intellectual preference view. In spite of his emphasis on the role of the practical judgment of the intellect in the act of choice, Aquinas insists that the human will is a wholly different power from the intellect, and that the will exercises the act of choice. As he views it, "essentially considered (*substantialiter*) choice is not an act of reason but of the will ... it is the act of an appetitive potency."[20]

Of the Mohammedan philosophers in the middle ages, Avicenna (eleventh century) has one of the most thoroughly developed psychologies. When he is commenting on, or paraphrasing, the *De Anima* of Aristotle, Avicenna stays rather close to the Aristotelian teaching. This means that volition is interpreted as an act of intellectual preference, accompanied by desire.[21] However, in his more personal works, Avicenna does talk about a faculty of will ($\supset ir\bar{a}da$) which has volition as its action. Goichon says of will in Avicenna:

It is nowhere defined, an interesting point in this system in which everything is necessary. Nevertheless, $\supset ir\bar{a}da$ (will) indicates a degree of initiative beyond $\supset i\underline{h}tiy\bar{a}r$ (choice) and is found almost exclusively as cause of movement; the same word designates the faculty and the act that springs from it, volition.[22]

Late thirteenth and early fourteenth-century Christian thinkers fall into two schools concerning will as a power: some stress its active character and resent any suggestion that volition is causally influenced by anything in the order of natural causes, other than will itself; others see the human will as a partly passive potency, subject to causal influence from the intellect, or from the object that is understood. The latter type of thinker usually adopts some version of an intellectual preference theory of volition. John the Dane, in a treatise on grammar written at the University of Paris about 1280, speaks of the intellect as "willing" and of will as *potestas rationalis*.[23] Godfrey of Fontaines taught that the human will cannot move itself, that the intellectually known object is the moving cause of volition, both in the order of efficient and of formal causality.[24] Godfrey seems to have been the closest approach to a supporter of the notion that willing is intellectual preference, to be found in the middle ages. In the same period (beginning of the fourteenth century), John Quidort, Nicholas Trivet and Thomas Sutton were "Thomists" who pushed the intellectualistic tendencies in Aquinas to an extremity. John Quidort raised the interesting question of what mode of activity would be possible to a will existing all by itself, in isolation as it were (*voluntas absoluta*). He decided that such a will, separated from the soul and its other powers, *could do nothing* by itself.[25]

If the foregoing Scholastic thinkers tended to stretch the power of intellect so that it might include volition, some of their opponents so exalted the power of the human will that they made it into a cognitive power! Both at Paris and at Oxford, in the fourteenth century, there were men who maintained that man's will (*voluntas*) not only performs the usual acts of wishing, intending, choosing and using the other potencies of man but that will also *knows* certain things. At Oxford, an Ockhamist named Adam Woodham is the focal point of this movement. Pierre d'Ailly (in Paris) discusses the view that every volition is a proposition on the optative mood (a vague anticipation of the emotive theory of contemporary ethics). An Augustinian theologian, Hugolinus de Malabranca, teaches that the human will has "experimental knowledge" of its own object and an effective memory of its past acts. Most of the writings of this group are unedited but have been studied by Konstantin Michalski.[26] These men usually deny that intellect and will are distinct powers; consequently, they fuse the functions of intellection and volition. It is not correct to say that they think of willing as mere intellectual preference; rather, they consider that understanding involves volition.

Modern philosophy provides several instances of the intellectualizing of volition. Thomas Hobbes speaks of will as the last action in a process of deliberation.

                                                              •

In deliberation, the last appetite, or aversion, immediately adhering to the action, or to the omission thereof, is what we call the WILL; the act, not the faculty, of willing.[27]

Deliberation goes on in the mind, and is a sort of thinking; however, it involves a succession of "appetites and aversions, hopes and fears, concerning one and the same thing."[28] It also includes a calculation of the consequences of a proposed action. In a way, this is a process of reasoning and will is a decision to terminate it. There appears to be an intellectual aspect to such calculation but it soon becomes evident that willing really comes under Hobbes' general view that all mental actions are internal motions in man's body. We shall treat Hobbes' meaning of will as a dynamic power theory, in Chapter Five.

With John Locke, the term "preference" comes into continued use, in speaking of a willed choice. He defines will as, "nothing but a power, or ability, to prefer or choose."[29] It is the mind which has this power:

This, at least, I think evident,—That we find in ourselves a power to begin or forbear, continue or end several actions of our minds, and motions of our bodies, barely *by a thought or preference of the mind* ordering, or as it were, commanding, the doing or not doing such or such a particular action. This power which the mind has thus to order the consideration of any idea, or the forbearing to consider it; or *to prefer* the motion of any part of the body to its rest, and *vice versa*, in any particular instance, is that which we call the Will.[30]

However, Locke's view of willing is not a clear example of an intellectual preference theory; his discussion of the role of feeling, desire and freedom, in personal activity, makes his explanation of willing much more complex than a mere intellectual judgment.

It is in Spinoza that we find the best historical example of a philosophy which equates willing with intellectual preference. He is much opposed to the view that will is free, with the "freedom of indifference." To Spinoza, this indifference theory would require that we grant to God or man the "power of acting without motive, or contrary to the strongest motive, the power of obeying or disobeying reason."[31] Of course, Spinoza's notion of freedom is predetermined by his initial definition: "That thing is called free, which exists solely by the necessity of its own nature, and of which the action is determined by itself alone."[32] It is clear that Spinoza has to develop a meaning of will that is not only different from that of the ordinary man but from that of the classical philosophers.

God's will is described by Spinoza, in the *Appendix* to Part I, of the *Ethics*. Like the divine intellect, the Will of God is not part of the divine nature or essence. The divine will is but a mode of the attribute of thought. As he puts it: "The actual intellect, whether it be finite or infinite, together with the will, desire, love, etc., must be referred to the natura naturata and not to the natura naturans."[33] Even the divine will, then, is more closely associated with intellect than with power; for the divine power belongs to God's essence.[34]

When, at the end of Part II of the *Ethics*, Spinoza comes to give a brief explanation of human will, he clearly treats it in function of his notion of divine volition. All human activities are wholly determined by their antecedent causes. There is desire (*cupiditas*) in man but this is not will (*voluntas*). Willing becomes the intellectual function of affirmation or denial.

In the mind there is no absolute or free will, but the mind is determined to this or that volition by a cause, which is also determined by another cause, and this again by another, and so on *ad infinitum*.

In the mind there is no volition or affirmation and negation excepting that which the idea, insofar as it is an idea, involves. . . . *Corollary.*—The will and the intellect are one and the same.[35]

Thus human will is not a matter of desire or feeling. This is emphasized by Spinoza in his discussion of Proposition 48:

By the will, I understand a faculty of affirming and denying, but not a desire; a faculty . . . by which the mind affirms and denies that which is true or false, and not a desire by which the mind seeks a thing or turns away from it.[36]

He had already made the same intellectual reduction of volition, in the earlier *Short Treatise on God, Man, and His Well-Being.*[37]

It is true that Spinoza later mentions volition as an aspect of the general *conatus* (or tendency of anything to persevere)[38] but this does not mean that the Spinozistic will is an appetite. To will means to make an intellectual judgment. This may be purely speculative, or mathematical, affirmation. One of Spinoza's examples of an individual volition is the action, "by which the mind affirms that the three angles of a triangle are equal to two right angles."[39] This is the theory of intellectual preference in its purest form. It is well characterized by Collins:

There is [for Spinoza] no real distinction between acts of knowing and willing. To will is nothing more than to affirm or deny that which is true or false in our ideas. This is a cognitive function and offers no ground of distinction for another class of powers or acts. Descartes had defended freedom by making judgment an act of will. Spinoza reduces the will to the cognitive function of judgment, making it subject to the same determinism governing all our cognitive operations.[40]

In spite of a generally intellectualistic attitude in his philosophy, Leibniz reacts to this extreme position of Spinoza and insists that there is a basic distinction between cognition and volition.[41] Leibniz does stress the role of rational motivation in volition, and uses Spinoza's word, *conatus*, in describing will; but he does not make willing an act of intellectual preference.

In point of fact, after Spinoza, there is no modern thinker who has so rigorously equated volition with intellection. Of course, the mediaeval and Scholastic teaching that the human will is a special faculty or potency of the soul is abandoned. Willing is often treated as a function of "mind" or understanding. Christian Wolff (1679–1754) produced textbooks in philosophy which popularized in academic circles the simplified rationalism of Descartes, Spinoza and Leibniz. Wolff made the theory of knowledge central in his systematization of philosophy. He taught that every man has a tendency to seek the good; if his idea of the good is obscure, the result is appetite; if his idea of the good is clear, the effect is will.[42] Another continental writer who helped to popularize a semi-intellectual view of willing was Jean Jacques Rousseau. He stressed the cognitive basis of feeling and volition, as the following passage from his novel, *Emile*, indicates.

I am only aware of will through the consciousness of my own will, and intelligence is no better known to me. When you ask me what is the cause which determines my will, it is my turn to ask what cause determines my judgment; for it is plain that these two causes are but one; and if you understand clearly that man is active in his judgments, that his intelligence is only the power to compare and judge, you will see that his freedom is only a similar power or one derived from this: *he chooses between good and evil as he judges between truth and falsehood;*

if his judgment is at fault, he chooses amiss. What then is the cause that determines his will? It is his judgment. And what is the cause that determines his judgment? It is his intelligence.[43]

Immanuel Kant is influenced by both Wolff and Rousseau. The Kantian view of will is complex; it is not a simple intellectual preference theory. However, there is one basic sense in which Kant deserves to be mentioned in this chapter. He frequently identified will with practical reason.

Rational beings alone have the faculty of acting according to the conception of laws—that is, according to principles, i.e. have a *will*. Since the deduction of actions from principles requires *reason*, the will is nothing but practical reason.[44]

It is the rational will (*der Wille*) that is thus made co-extensive with practical reason, not the elective will (*die Willkür*).

In the early period of philosophy in the United States, Jonathan Edwards is the outstanding writer on the meaning of will. His view is somewhat intellectualistic. Most thinkers who have tended to identify willing with an act of intellectual preference have taken choice as the central function of volition. Edwards does this: "The faculty of the will is that faculty or power or principle of mind by which it is capable of choosing: an act of the will is the same as an act of choosing or choice."[45] He explains that the will is always determined in its choice by the strongest motive.[46] The motivation may be complex, many particular things may be operative, but it is essential that such motives be grasped by the mind or intelligence of the voluntary agent.

Edwards was regarded, and violently opposed, by many religious writers in the eighteenth and nineteenth centuries, as an advocate of determinism and a destroyer of freedom.

Actually, his position may be no more deterministic than that of Thomas Aquinas. Edwards argued that there must always be some reason or cause for an intelligent act of choice. As he sees it:

> in every act of will there is an an act of choice; that in every volition there is a preference, or a prevailing inclination of the soul, whereby the soul, at that instant, is out of a state of perfect indifference, with respect to the direct object of the volition. So that in every act, or going forth of the will, there is some preponderation of the mind or inclination, one way rather than another. . . .
>
> Things that exist in the view of the mind, have their strength, tendency or advantage to move or excite its will . . . whatever is perceived or apprehended by an intelligent and voluntary agent, which has the nature and influence of a motive to volition or choice, is considered or viewed as good . . . the will always is as the greatest apparent good is.[47]

From this one may conclude that Jonathan Edwards closely related volitional choice to the act of intelligent preference. This does not mean that he reduced volition to the action of the speculative understanding (as did Spinoza). Edwards sometimes speaks of a moral faculty, or sense, and it is difficult to determine what are its relations with ordinary intelligence.[48] It is clear that Edwards' critics among the Faculty Psychologists of the nineteenth century felt that he neglected the characteristic of activity which they thought essential to the meaning of will.[49]

With the development of a pragmatic theory of human knowledge and truth, in twentieth-century American thought, the field of cognition seems to coalesce with that of volition. As a consequence, many pragmatists make very little difference between a preferential judgment and a volitional decision to act in a certain way. What has happened in pragmatism is not so much that willing has been interpreted as a cognitive function but rather that knowing has been shifted into the area of volitional activity. In this sense, American pragmatism and instrumentalism has rather closely associated willing with intelligent decision.

William James' theory of attention is a case in point. In his early work, *Principles of Psychology*, he says:

The only resistance which our will can possibly experience is the resistance which . . . an idea offers to being attended to at all. To attend to it is the volitional act, and the only inward volitional act which we ever perform. . . . Volition is primarily a relation, not between our Self and extra-mental matter (as many philosophers still maintain), but between our Self and our own states of mind.[50]

At times, James suggests that willing is little more than the continuity and dominance of a certain "idea" of action. This view is expressed in cognitive terms and approximates to the preference theory. A typical statement of this view is the following: "whether or not there be anything else in the mind at the moment when we consciously will a certain act, a mental conception made up of memory-images of these sensations, defining which special act it is, must be there."[51] However, James' explanation of human willing is more complex than an intellectual preference theory. He stressed the importance of a "feeling of effort"[52] and also the physiological basis of ideo-motor activity.[53] In his later writings, will is treated as a spring, or trigger, for the release of man's deepest energies.[54] This "power" aspect of James' theory will be considered later, in Chapter Five.

Josiah Royce also closely integrates willing with knowing,

and approves of this tendency in the pragmatic movement. In one lengthy passage he offers a view of will that is not far removed from James' "Will to Believe."

I have myself long since maintained [Royce says] that there is a logic of the will, just as truly as there is a logic of the intellect. Personally, I go further still. I assert: all logic is the logic of the will. There is no pure intellect. Thought is a mode of action, a mode of action distinguished from other modes mainly by its internal clearness of self-consciousness, by its relatively free control of its own procedure, and by the universality, the impersonal fairness and obviousness of its aims and of its motives. . . . General assertions about the meaning of our ideas are reflective acts whereby we acknowledge and accept certain ruling principles of action. And in respect of all these aspects of doctrine I find myself at one with recent voluntarism, whether the latter takes the form of instrumentalism, or insists upon some more individualistic theory of truth. But for my part, in spite, or in fact because of this my voluntarism, I cannot rest in any mere relativism. Individualism is right in saying, 'I will to credit this or that opinion.' But individualism is wrong in supposing that I can ever be content with my own will in as far as it is merely an individual will. The will, to my mind, is nothing but a thirst for a complete and conscious self-possession, for fullness of life. And in terms of this its central motive, the will defines the truth that it endlessly seeks as a truth that possesses completeness, totality, self-possession, and therefore absoluteness.[55]

This highly personal statement of Royce's shows how the will came to be associated with the quest for true knowledge, in American philosophy of the early twentieth century. It even helps us to understand that John Dewey's development from an early idealism to instrumentalism was not as abrupt as some interpreters would have us think, and that such a move was far from an isolated phenomenon in American thought. The view that an idea can be a product of will is a recurrent theme in Royce's great work, *The World and the Individual*.

Every idea is as much a volitional process as it is an intellectual process. It may well or ill represent or correspond to something not itself, but it must, in any case, make more or less clearly articulate its own present purpose. The constructive character of all mathematical ideas, the sense of current control which accompanies all definite thinking processes, the momentary purposes more or less imperfectly fulfilled whenever we conceive anything,—these are evidences of what is essential to the processes of ideation. Volition is as manifest in counting objects as in singing tunes, in conceiving physical laws as in directing the destinies of nations, in laboratory experiments as in artistic productions, in contemplating as in fighting. The embodied purpose, the internal meaning, of the instant's act, is thus a *conditio sine qua non* for all external meaning and for all truth.[56]

In John Dewey's early psychology, will is described as the relation between the subjective and the objective in consciousness, where feeling is subjective and knowledge objective.[57] As he moved away from idealism, Dewey embraced more of the naturalistic psychology of James. Primitive impulses are organized and re-directed by habits. Habit-formation becomes a central feature of conscious life. In *Human Nature and Conduct*, Dewey equates will with habit. "Habit means special sensitiveness or accessibility to certain classes of stimuli, standing predilections and aversions, rather than bare recurrence of specific acts. It means will."[58] Choice is taken as the typical act of volition and is described in terms of preference. "It [choice] is the emergence of a unified preference out of competing preferences."[59] The locus of the interplay of competing preferences is the imagination. So, choosing is a "hitting in imagination upon an object which furnishes an adequate stimulus to the recovery of overt action."[60] There is an element of judgment involved; the elective judgment is made, "in the light of the consequences of the act."[61] Personal freedom is the power of varied and flexible growth, of change of disposition and character, that springs from intelligent choice.[62]

Verbally then, the instrumentalist theory of volition is quite properly called an intellectual preference view. In its actual meaning, however, Dewey's "will" is but one aspect of a sophisticated account of motivation and decision as the immediate and concomitant factors of conscious human activity. This is not an intellectualism, in the older and classical sense of a purely cognitive function, but is (as Royce fully realized) a type of voluntarism.

In recent thinking, one of the nearest approaches to a purely intellectual theory of willing is found in the literature of decision-making and games theory.[63] Here, will becomes a matter of calculating by statistical methods the most likely answer to a problem. It is assumed that most practical problems, or games, present a rather limited number of methods of solution. Once these possibilities have been determined, it is a rather simple statistical operation to select the solution which will most probably work in the given circumstances. This answer is the best decision or choice. One's "will" is simply such an end-directed decision. As L. Von Mises states it: "Human action is purposeful behavior. Or we may say: Action is will put into operation and transformed into an agency, is aiming at ends and goals."[64] This notion that willing is essentially a statistical process of decision-making has gained widespread acceptance in recent works in economics and social psychology.[65]

By way of conclusion, we may observe that this way of

speaking about will, as intellectual preference, has been found to have some acceptance in nearly all periods of Western thought. It appears to make volition into a cognitive function. In less extreme forms, willing is an activity of mind that is predetermined by the cognitive presentation of, or attention to, the greatest known good. To people who regard the will as a distinct power of man, or who see volitional activity in any of the distinctive ways which are to be described in the next seven chapters, this intellectualist meaning of will appears to take away all distinctive meaning from the term. Spinoza pushed the theory to its ultimate, when he pointed out that there is no difference between intellect and will.

NOTES

1. Plato, *Protagoras*, 361, for the concluding summary; cf. Xenophon, *Memorabilia*, III, 9, 4.

2. Aristotle, *Nicomachean Ethics*, VII, 2, 1145b25.

3. Plato, *Republic*, IV, 435–442; VI, 514A; VIII, 550A; IX, 571, 580E, 581; *Timaeus*, 69E–72, 89E; *Phaedrus*, 246–248.

4. *Gorgias*, 466D.

5. *Republic*, X, 616–619; see the translation and notes in F. M. Cornford, *The Republic of Plato* (New York-London, Oxford University Press, 1956), pp. 355–359.

6. See the comment in R. L. Nettleship, *Lectures on the Republic of Plato* (London: Macmillan, 1922), pp. 359–361.

7. R. E. Brennan, *Thomistic Psychology* (New York: Macmillan, 1941), pp. 28–29 (in a chapter entitled: "The Psychology of Aristotle").

8. W. D. Ross, *Aristotle* (London: Methuen, 1923), pp. 199–200.

9. Aristotle, *De Anima*, III, 3–5, 427a16–430a25, contains the analysis which led to the medieval theories of potential and agent intellects.

10. *Ibid.*, 9, 432b4–7.

11. *Ibid.*, 10, 433a21. (The translations are from *The Basic Works of Aristotle*, ed. R. McKeon, New York: Random House, 1941, pp. 596, 598.)

12. Cf. *Rhetoric*, I, 10, 1369a3, which states that *boulesis* "is an *orexis* for the good."

13. St. Thomas Aquinas, *In Aristotelis libros De Anima*, lib. III, lect. 14 (ad loc. cit.): "Erunt igitur *tres appetitus* in anima, *subjecto differentes*, secundum praedictam divisionem." (Italics added.)

14. See *Nic. Ethics*, III, 1, 1109b28–1111b3.

15. *Ibid.*, cc. 1–4, 1110b32–1113b1.

16. *Ibid.*, VI, 2, 1139b3.

17. J. Von Arnim, *Stoicorum veterum fragmenta* (Leipzig, 1914), I, 143; citing Nemesius' report on Zeno.

18. M. T. Cicero, *Disp. Tusc.*, IV, 6; the translation is from *The Academic Questions, De Finibus, and Tusculan Disputations*, trans. C. D. Yonge (London: Bohn, 1853), p. 403.

19. For the Latin see: Thémistius, *Commentaire sur le traité de l'âme d'Aristote*, traduction de Guillaume de Moerbeke, éd. par G. Verbeke (Louvain-Paris: Nauwelaerts, 1957). The word, *voluntas*, is used for *boulesis*, pp. 87, line 54; 265, line 47; 271, lines 1–5.

20. St. Thomas Aquinas, *Summa Theologiae*, I–II, 13, 1, c., ad fin.

21. Avicenna, *Liber Sextus Naturalium* (*De Anima*) (Venetiis, 1509); in the transcription (of this Latin version of Dominic Gundissalinus and John Avendeath) made by G. P. Klubertanz (St. Louis: *The Modern Schoolman*, 1949) see c. 4–5, pp. 17–24.

22. A. M. Goichon, *Lexique de la langue philosophique d'Ibn Sīnā* (Paris: Desclée de Brouwer, 1938), p. 145, n. 282; for "choice" see p. 115, n. 234.

23. John the Dane, *Summa Grammatica*, ed. A. Otto, 2 vols. (Copenhagen: G. E. C. Gad, 1955), II, 233: "Deinde intellectus volens id quod intellexit alii significari, imponit vocem ad significandum." Cf. vol. I, 62: "Major patet, quia voluntas, que est potestas rationalis, est ad oppositum seu ad utrumlibet."

24. Godefrey, *Quodlibeta*, VI, q. 11 (ed. *Les Philosophes Belges*, par M. de Wulf et al., Louvain: Institut Supérieur, 1904–1937, tome III, 221–224). For further references, see R. J. Arway, "A Half-Century of Research on Godfrey of Fontaines," *New Scholasticism*, XXXVI, 2 (1962), 192–218; on Godfrey's psychology of will, see pp. 211–217.

25. John of Paris, *Quodlibetum I*, q. V: "Quaeritur utrum Deus posset facere voluntatem sine anima." The text is edited in: A. J. Heiman, "The First Quodlibet of Jean Quidort," in *Nine Mediaeval*

Thinkers (Toronto: Pontifical Institute of Mediaeval Studies, 1955), pp. 279–280, where John says of such a "separated" will, "non poterit velle quia deest sibi principium actionis et volitionis."

26. K. Michalski, "Le Problème de la volonté à Oxford et à Paris au XIVe siècle," *Commentariorum Societatis Philosophicae Polonorum,* II (Limberg, 1937), 233–365. For the very distinctive position of Hugolinus, see p. 279.

27. T. Hobbes, *Leviathan,* I, 6 (*English Works,* ed. W. Molesworth, 11 vols., London: Bohn and Longmans, 1839–1845, III, 49).

28. *Ibid.*

29. J. Locke, *Essay concerning Human Understanding,* II, 21, 7, (ed. A. C. Fraser, 2 vols., New York: Dover, 1959, I, 314).

30. *Ibid.,* n. 73; ed. Fraser, I, 367. (Italics added.)

31. The quotation is from R. A. Duff, *Spinoza's Political and Ethical Philosophy* (Glasgow: Maclehose and Sons, 1903), p. 37.

32. B. Spinoza, *Ethics,* Part I, def. VII; (in *The Works of Spinoza,* 2 vols., trans. by R. H. M. Elwes, London: Bell, 1883–1884, II, 45). Cf. *Epist.* 62: "I place freedom not in free decision but in free necessity." (Elwes, I, 390.)

33. *Ethics,* I, prop. 31.

34. *Ibid.,* prop. 34.

35. *Ibid.,* II, prop. 48–49.

36. *Ibid.,* prop. 48.

37. In the *Short Treatise,* II, 16 (written five or more years before the *Ethics*), Spinoza had said: "the power to affirm and deny is called will"; then he adds that desire "is the inclination which the soul has towards something which it chooses as a good."

38. *Ethics,* III, prop. 59.

39. *Ibid.,* II, prop. 49.

40. J. Collins, *A History of Modern European Philosophy* (Milwaukee: Bruce, 1954), pp. 234–235.

41. G. W. Leibniz *Refutation of Spinoza,* in *Leibniz Selections,* ed. P. Wiener (New York: Scribner, 1951), p. 495.

42. See A. Alexander, *Theories of the Will in the History of Philosophy* (New York: Scribner, 1898), pp. 254–255, citing Wolff, *Vernünftige Gedanken.*

43. J. J. Rousseau, *Emile,* trans. Barbara Foxley (New York, Dutton, 1948), p. 243.

44. I. Kant, *Fundamental Principles of the Metaphysic of Morals,* sect. II (in T. K. Abbott, *Kant's Theory of Ethics,* London: Longmans, Green, 1909, p. 30).

45. J. Edwards, *Freedom of the Will*, ed. Paul Ramsey (New Haven: Yale University Press, 1957), p. 137.

46. *Ibid.*, p. 141.

47. *Ibid.*, pp. 137, 142.

48. On the moral faculty, see *ibid.*, p. 165.

49. See Albert T. Bledsoe, *An Examination of President Edwards' Inquiry into the Freedom of the Will* (Philadelphia, 1845), pp. 101–102; cf. H. W. Schneider, *A History of American Philosophy* (New York: Columbia University Press, 1946), p. 236.

50. W. James, *Principles of Psychology*, 2 vols. (New York: Holt, 1907), vol. II, pp. 567–568.

51. *Ibid.*, II, 492.

52. W. James, "What the Will Effects," *Scribner's Magazine*, III (1888), 240–250.

53. Cf. O. F. Kraushaar, "What James' Philosophical Orientation Owed to Lotze," *Philosophical Review*, 47 (1938), 517–526.

54. See the Essay: "The Energies of Man," in *Memories and Studies* (New York: Longmans, Green, 1911); of which an abbreviation was printed, under the title: "How To Increase Your Energy," in *Reader's Digest*, Oct. 1961, pp. 40–42. It was originally an address to the American Philosophical Association, in 1906.

55. J. Royce, "The Problem of Truth," Essay IV in *William James and Other Essays* (New York: Macmillan, 1911), p. 234.

56. J. Royce, *The World and the Individual*, 2 vols. (New York: Macmillan, 1900–1901); reprinted, New York: Dover, 1959, p. 311.

57. J. Dewey, *Psychology* (New York: Harper, 3rd. ed., 1897), p. 23.

58. *Human Nature and Conduct* (New York: Holt, 1922), p. 42; cf. p. 52: "will, as we have seen, means, in the concrete, habits."

59. *Ibid.*, p. 193.

60. *Ibid.*, p. 192.

61. *Ibid.*, p. 120.

62. *Philosophy and Civilization* (New York: Minton, Balch, 1931), p. 295.

63. See: J. Von Neumann and O. Morgenstern, *Theory of Games and Economic Behavior* (Princeton, N.J.: Princeton University Press, 1947); H. Kuhn, *Contributions to the Theory of Games* (Princeton, N.J.: Princeton University Press, 1950); L. Von Mises, *Human Action. A Treatise on Economics* (New Haven: Yale University Press, 1949); and two basic mathematical works: A. Wald, *Statistical Decision Functions* (New York: Wiley, 1950); J. C. C. McKinsey,

Introduction to the Theory of Games (New York: McGraw-Hill, 1952).

64. Von Mises, *op. cit.*, p. 11.

65. The works of Von Neumann and Von Mises show some of the economic applications. For typical use in social psychology, see: Lewin, Dembo, Festinger and Sears, "Level of Aspiration," in *Personality and the Behavior Disorders* (New York: Ronald Press, 1944), vol. I, 333–378; and S. E. Asch, *Social Psychology* (New York: Prentice-Hall, 1952), pp. 511–623.

Will as Rational Appetite

Will as Rational Appetite

A SECOND THEORY of will interprets volition as a special type of appetition. In this view, will is regarded as a psychic power enabling its possessor to incline toward objects intellectually apprehended as goods, and to tend away from objects intellectually known as evils. The actions of such a will are elicited by prior or concomitant acts of intellectual cognition: not in the sense that understanding efficiently produces volitions but rather that understanding, or its known objects, may provide the final and/or formal causality which attracts and/or specifies the movements which intellectual appetite itself makes in response to known ends or forms. Nothing is willed that is not somewhat understood but volition is an entirely different kind of activity from cognition.

This is a teleological interpretation of will functions. Final causality is important to this theory. Not only is every kind of being considered to have an end, or good, to which it naturally tends in its continued existence, but also the various operative potencies of each being are thought of as naturally inclining toward certain functions and objects which constitute the natural goals of these powers. Biological, sensory and intellectual levels of appetitive functions in man, for instance, are considered to be directed toward ends on these three different levels. Appetites, or capacities to be attracted to appropriate ends, are distinguished on all three levels. In-

tellectual appetition (the general name for all forms of volition) is specifically different from both biological instincts
and sensory desires, loves and pleasures. What so distinguishes
will is the claim that its objects, or ends, must be *intellectually*
or *rationally* known. According to this theory, a person might
incline in sensory appetition toward the individual pleasure
of eating an apple but he would *will* (or desire by intellectual
appetition) the understood goodness of the vitamins thought
to be present in the apple. In most forms of the intellectual
appetite theory, the objects of will are regarded as *universal*
goods.

Formal causality is also essential to this interpretation of
volition. That is to say: each volition must be of some definite
type; one wills an end or object of a certain kind. The character or kind of volition is specified (not efficiently produced)
by the kind of intellectual cognition with which it is associated. It will be seen that motivation, in the case of an intellectual appetite theory of will, is a complex matter. A motive
is not something that efficiently *pushes* the will toward action
but is an end which stimulates as a good to be attained or an
evil to be avoided. Moreover, motivation may also be viewed
in terms of formal causality: in this sense the motive for a
will function may include the cognitive apprehension of a
certain way of desiring or effectuating one's desires. Thus
one might will peace, as an intellectual objective, but a more
definite volition to do something to accomplish peace might
await the intellectual discovery of a method (or formal way)
of attaining peace. This discovery could then motivate another
volition, after the fashion of a formal cause specifying the
activity of a basic efficient cause which is the will itself.

St. Thomas Aquinas is the thinker who has, perhaps, offered
the most highly developed analysis of volition as rational appetition. There are anticipations of the theory in ancient and

early medieval philosophy. Apart from later Thomists and Scholastic thinkers, there are not many thinkers in the modern period who have so understood will. This is partly due to the dropping out of the metaphysical theories of final and formal causality and the tendency of modern philosophers to think of all causes as agents, as efficient producers of effects. However, there are some noteworthy examples of modern philosophers who have retained at least some aspects of the rational appetite view. Leibniz is one such. It should be obvious that this explanation of willing is rooted in a whole philosophy of nature, metaphysics, and psychology which cannot be explained here.

The concept of psychic appetition has been noted (in the preceding chapter) as present in the *orexis* theory of Aristotle. We have seen that he thought that there is but one general orectic power in man. Post-Aristotelian psychology among the Greeks offers various *schemata* of the powers of man which show a growing awareness of the difference between functions which man may personally control and those which are not subject to such control. A typical table is found in Panaetius of Rhodes (180–110 B.C.) who introduced Stoicism to Rome. He names seven psychic functions that are subject to choice (*proairesis*) and five vital functions that are not.[1] There is no will, as such, in this schematism but Panaetius distinguishes a power of movement *along with desire* from a general motor capacity of the whole living body. *Boulesis* is not mentioned in connection with this table.

In his fourth *Ennead*, Plotinus records what he knew of such analyses of the powers of man. At one point he lists a modification of the Aristotelian table of powers, naming sense, motor, desiderative (*horme*), imaginative and rational powers (*dynameis*). Immediately following reason (*ton logon*) he puts what appears to be another appetitive power (*horme kai orexis*).² It would appear that by this time (third century A.D.) a distinction was being made between sensory appetition and rational appetition.

A Greek Father of the Church, St. John Damascene, compiled a good deal of this speculation on the powers of man, in a section of his eighth-century treatise, *The Source of Knowledge*. In the middle of the twelfth century, this last part of the work was translated into Latin, by Burgundio of Pisa, under the title, *De fide orthodoxa* (*On the Right Faith*).³ In this Latin form the work became very influential and helped to popularize an appetitive theory of will. We shall quote the key text from this work in full, reminding the reader that it is from an imperfect Latin translation of a Greek text which is not entirely clear. Damascene wrote:

It should be noted that our soul has two kinds of powers, some are cognitive, others vital (*zoticas*). Now the cognitive ones are: understanding, mind, opinion, imagination, sense. The vital or appetitive powers are *consilium* [a mistranslation of *boulesis*, which means wish or will] and choice (*proairesis*). It should also be noted that there is naturally present in the soul an appetitive power which is according to nature, and it is inclining toward all the things that are associated substantially with its nature: this is called will [*voluntas* in Latin, *thelesis* in Greek]. For substance inclines (*appetit*) to be, to live, and to be moved, according to sense and intellect, craving its own natural or complete being. Therefore, they describe this natural will (*thelema*) in this way: the will (*thelema*), i.e. *voluntas*, is itself natural, vital and reasonable, an appetite for all the components of nature, a simple power (*virtus*); there is another appetite for other things and it is not rational, nor is it called will (*voluntas—thelesis*), that is to say, the natural and rational appetite of anything. In fact, there is present in the soul of man a power of rational appetition (*virtus rationabiliter appetendi*). Since it is a natural movement, this rational appetite for anything is called *boulesis* [*bulisis* in the Latin], i.e. will. For *boulesis*, i.e. will, is a rational appetite and desire belonging to anything. It is called *boulesis*, both in regard to things within our power and things that are not, that is, in regard to possible and impossible objectives.[4]

The main point to note in the foregoing text from John Damascene is that (in the twelfth-century Burgundian translation) it introduces into Latin the terminology of *rational appetition*. As far as the psychology of the passage is concerned, two things should be stressed. First, two levels of appetite are attributed to man, irrational and rational.[5] This is the proximate source of the thirteenth-century Scholastic distinction between plural appetitive powers in man. Second, John Damascene is compiling this psychology from two earlier Greek Christian sources: Nemesius' treatise *On the Nature of Man*, and Maximus the Confessor's *Opuscula Theologica ad Marinum*.[6] Although Nemesius' treatise was translated into Latin, in both the eleventh and the twelfth centuries, and exerted some influence on later theories of willing,[7] the Scholastic theory that there are two kinds of psychic appetite in man (sensory and rational) stems chiefly from John Damascene. St. Thomas Aquinas is indebted to Damascene for his views on the difference between willing an end and willing a means to an end, and for the seeds of his famous analysis of the stages in the volitional process. The distinction between *natural* and *deliberated* movements of will is also Damascenian.

Psychology is a subject to which medieval Mohammedan scholars devoted much attention. They knew Aristotle's treatise *On the Soul* long before Christian thinkers had it in Latin. One might expect to find a theory of rational appetite in the Arabic literature of the ninth to the twelfth centuries but, actually, these writers say very little about a distinct power of intellectual appetition in man. In Avicenna's paraphrase of the Aristotelian *De Anima*, sensory and intellectual powers (*vires*, in the Latin version) are distinguished. On the level of sensory functions, cognitive powers are distinguished from appetitive ones. On the rational level, there is a difference between the powers of knowing and of acting (*vires sciendi et agendi*).[8] However, both are called *intellectus* (understanding) and there is no formal treatment of a power of will, considered as an intellectual appetite.

In his more personal works, Avicenna speaks of a sensible will and an intellectual will. He also differentiates between reflective and instinctive choice.[9] But these precisions were not influential in the general development of Western thinking on will. It is rather significant that, in the *De Anima* of Gundissalinus (the Latin translator of Avicenna, in the twelfth century), there is no mention of will (*voluntas*) in the listing of the rational powers of the human soul.[10]

Averroes also says very little about human will. We now have good editions of his commentaries on the psychological works of Aristotle.[11] They contain no developed theory of will as rational appetite. Both Avicenna and Averroes speak of volition as desire stemming from a cognitive apprehension in the imagination. Thus Averroes states rather vaguely: "will is nothing else than a desire motivated in us as a consequence of an imagination or a judgment."[12] In his report of Avicenna's views on how a person voluntarily moves his hand, Algazel says: "the movement of the hand comes from the power of desire (*ex virtute desiderii*), and the movement of the power of desire comes from the power of imagination."[13] We may conclude that medieval Mohammedan psychology does not offer a definite theory of intellectual appetition, although it comes at least as close as Aristotle did to this theory of will.

Christian psychology in the Latin works of the twelfth century is innocent of Aristotelian complexities. Various modifications of Augustine's notion of *voluntas* (the whole soul *as active*) are found. Gilbert of Poitiers, for instance, distinguishes three levels of psychic life in man: the lowest is soul (*anima*), the middle level is spirit (*spiritus*), the highest is mind (*mens*). Each is called a virtual part of man and the soul (*anima*) is said to have its cognitive and appetitive capacity (the latter being *sensualitas*), while the mind (*mens*) has its cognitive power (*intellectus*) and its appetitive power (*voluntas*).[14] Similarly, Hugh of Saint Victor holds that there are three levels of human cognition (cogitation, meditation and contemplation) and places a "will" on each level.[15] Such psychologies contain the seeds of a theory of intellectual appetite but the theory does not reach its full growth until the thirteenth century.

There is no question that the human will was regarded as a special power of rational appetition by many of the predecessors of St. Thomas Aquinas. Several things contributed to this development in early thirteenth-century psychology. First of all, there was a gradual movement toward a faculty psychology, under the influence of the new translations of the psychological writings of Aristotle.[16] The notion that the human soul is the immediate agency of all its actions (Augustine's *voluntas*) is replaced in many thinkers by the view that specifically distinct functions of man are to be attributed to a plurality of operative potencies.[17] Secondly, discussions of the nature of free choice (*liberum arbitrium*) led to further precisions concerning the role of reason, intellect and will in human activity.[18] A third influence may be found in the views of John Damascene, who was much quoted in the thirteenth century.[19]

Writing during the 1240's, Albert the Great describes the human will as the rational appetite of the soul.[20] In general, he understands "appetite" to mean any inclination toward what is fitting.[21] More particularly, psychic appetites are powers whereby the agent inclines toward (or away from) known objects. Since there are two levels of human knowledge, sensory and intellectual, the former apprehending individual objects or qualities and the latter apprehending universal objects, Albert says that sensory appetition has sensible things as its objects, and that intellectual appetition (will) has intelligible, universal items as its objects. Appetite is a generic name; one of its species is will.[22] The views of Albert, concerning will, are not fundamentally different from those of his pupil, Thomas Aquinas.

Another representative thinker who wrote before St. Thomas is St. Bonaventure. His psychology is somewhat different from the Thomistic but, as far as this description of the human will is concerned, Bonaventure is in general agreement. He says that there are three kinds of appetite in man, natural (or physical), sensual and rational.[23] The last is called will (*voluntas*) and its objects are intellectually apprehended goods. Generally speaking, Bonaventure is not as insistent as Aquinas on the real distinction of the soul from its potencies, and on the differentiation of these potencies among themselves. However, he quite clearly teaches that will is a separate power of rational appetition. The following text shows that he knows Aristotle's teaching and interprets it much as Aquinas is to understand it within a few years:

The Philosopher [Aristotle], as is evident in *De Anima*, III, in the chapter on the mover [c. 7], makes a difference between practical intellect and appetite, and he never says that understanding becomes appetite; rather, he properly says that speculative understanding becomes practical, for the same intellect and potency which directs in the process of consideration afterwards regulates in the process of acting. Now, will (*voluntas*) is not the practical intellect but is ratiocinative appetite; and so, it does not follow from this that reason simply becomes will by extension, or that intellect becomes an affective power.[24]

Thomas Aquinas is doubtless the outstanding representative in Western thought of the view that man's will is a special power of rational appetition. His theory of will is very detailed and cannot be fully analyzed here.[25] Volition is treated by Aquinas in most of his major works: the *Commentary on the Sentences*, Book II, d. 25 (A.D. 1256); the *Questions on Truth*, q. 22 (A.D. 1256–1259); the *Questions on Evil*, q.6 (A.D. 1270?); the *Summa of Theology*, Part I, q. 82 (A.D. 1265–1269) and Part I–II qq. 6–17 (A.D. 1270). The view of will is basically the same, throughout, though it appears that Aquinas placed a little more stress on the *activity* of the human will, in his later works, though he never denied that it is a partly passive potency.[26] Our expositions of his theory will not attempt to follow the minute changes in his teaching but will deal with volition as described in the mature writings.

First of all, cognition and appetition are understood by Aquinas to be utterly different psychic activities. This distinction is so basic that he almost supposes that his readers will naturally grant it. Knowing is an activity which terminates inside the knower: the cognitive union of knower and thing known results in the knower "becoming" the thing known, not physically but by an intentional identification. On the other hand, appetition means an act of seeking, of tending toward, a thing that is in some sense desired.[27] The result of knowing is a perfection of the knowing power itself; the result of appetition is the use of some power other than appetite for the attainment (*adeptio*) of the thing that is desired.[28] In relation to the person, cognition is an *ingoing* activity from the thing known; appetition is an *outgoing* activity toward the thing desired.[29]

Three types of appetition are distinguished by St. Thomas, the third being identical with volition. He explains these three levels in the following text:

Since every inclination is the result of a form, natural appetite results from a form existing in nature [he is thinking of an example such as the tending of iron filings toward a magnet], but a sensory appetite or even an intellectual or rational appetite (which is called will) is the result of an apprehended form. Thus that toward which a natural appetite tends is some good thing existing in reality; and that toward which a psychic or volitional appetite tends is an apprehended good.[30]

Thus, there are what might be called physical, sensory and intellectual levels of appetition. The human will is the psychic power enabling a person to tend toward or away from something apprehended intellectually as good or evil.

Sensory and intellectual appetition are not regarded as functions of the same power, nor have they the same objects. Through sense cognition individual things are known as attractive or repellent. Appetitive responses to these sensitively perceived goods or evils are considered passions of the sensory appetites.[31] Such emotional desires and aversions are not attributed to the will. Intellectual cognition has as its objects the universal characteristics of reality. Goods and evils of this universal type are the objects of intellectual appetition, or will. To wish for peace or health would be an act of willing; to desire a drink of water, when thirsty, would be an act of sensory appetition. Thomas Aquinas would say that one could also *will* to drink water—but this volition would have some universal "reason why" it is willed, for the sake of good health, say.

The objects of volition are also divided, according to St. Thomas, into ends and means. Ends of volition are intelligible goods that are desired for their own sake. Means are intelligible goods that are desired for the sake of something else, namely an end. The reason why (*propter quod*) an end is willed is its own intrinsic goodness but the reason why a means is willed is something other than the means. A person might will to undergo a painful surgical operation for the sake of regaining good health: the operation is the means and good health is the end. Upon reflection, many ends are recognized as means to a more remote, or intrinsically good, end. Obviously, this theory of will requires that there be an ultimate end, desired for its own sake alone. In several works (notably the Third Book of the *Summa contra Gentiles* and in the first five questions of the *Summa of Theology*, I–II), Aquinas argues that there is one such ultimate end for all men. It is identified as the Perfect Good, or God.[32]

One meaning of nature, according to Aquinas, designates whatever substance a being is.[33] Thus a dog is one kind of substance with its special functions and tendencies, and a man is a different kind of substance. If a man is a rational substance, then his natural inclination will be directed to any and every sort of rationally apprehended good. Since "will" means rational appetite, the generic object of volition is the good in general. For such an object, man has a "natural" desire: this means that man necessarily wills that which is apprehended as good, with no admixture of evil. This natural volition (*voluntas ut natura*) is not free. Here is how St. Thomas argues the point, after giving the meaning of nature which was stated at the beginning of this paragraph:

Thus, according to this meaning of nature, the first principle of all items that belong to a thing must be natural. This is quite evident in reference to the intellect, for the principles of intellectual knowledge are naturally known. Likewise, the principle [or starting point] of volitional functions ought to be something that is naturally willed. Now, this is the good in general (*bonum in communi*) toward which the will naturally inclines, just as every potency inclines to its object. It is also the ultimate end, for it is situated among objects of appetition in the same way that first principles are among objects of understanding. In general, it includes all those things that are suitable to the willing agent, according to his nature. For, by willing, we desire not only those goods that belong to the will as a potency but also those that are appropriate to each of the other powers and to the whole man. Hence a man naturally wills not only the object of his will but also the other goods that are suitable to the other potencies: the knowledge of what is true, which is fitting for the intellect; and to exist and to live, and similar things that have to do with maintaining the natural continuity of our existence. All of these are included within the object of the will, as particular goods.[34]

So, it is important to note that the Thomistic theory of will does not suggest that all volitions are free. Instead, it is essential to the view that some movements of human willing be recognized as determined by the nature of man.[35] Volitional functioning in man is initiated by certain automatic inclinations toward the good in general, or toward objects that are apprehended intellectually as unmixed with evil. Another kind of volitions are directed to objects that are not so clearly good for man. On such matters, a person may deliberate. The objects are weighed in the balance of the understanding and, if judged good under given circumstances, they may be willed also. Such willing is called deliberate (*voluntas deliberata*) and it is the kind of volition that is free. "Many particular goods are included under the good in general; to these no volition is determined."[36]

Further analysis suggests to Thomas Aquinas the distinction between the exercise of the act of willing and the specification of the will-act (*exercitium actus . . . specificationem actus*).[37] The person may decide to will or not to will (this is a question of exercising the will or not doing so); or having decided to perform a will-act, he may further consider what kind of object he may will. From the point of view of exercising the will, Aquinas thinks that no man is necessitated by any object: it is always possible to refrain from thinking of something and consequently from actually willing. In regard to the specification of the will-act, some purely good objects do determine the will-act (as we have seen above) and other particular goods which are imperfectly good can be either willed or rejected. Freedom of choice lies in the order of specification. St. Thomas summarizes this teaching, as follows:

The ultimate end moves the will necessarily, because it is a perfect good. The same is true of those goods that are directed to this end as means without which the end could not be attained, goods such as to exist and to live, and the like. Other objects, however, without which the end could be attained, are not necessarily willed by the person who wills the end; just as conclusions that are not necessary for the truth of the principles do not have to be accepted by the person who accepts the principles.[38]

From the foregoing, it should be obvious why St. Thomas almost never speaks of free will (*libera voluntas*) and practically always discusses man's freedom in terms of free choice (*liberum arbitrium*) of means. The act of free choice or election (*electio*) is a combined activity of intellect and will, in which man judges intellectually what is good in the order of imperfect goods and commits himself volitionally to his preference. Choice is an act of the human will, performed under the specifying direction of the human intellect.[39] Materially, choice belongs to the will; formally, it pertains to reason. In one text, Aquinas suggests that *willing* (*velle*, simple appetition of an intelligible end) is related to *choosing* (*eligere*, inclining to something for the sake of another) as *understanding* (*intelligere*, simple apprehension) is to *reasoning* (*ratiocinari*, moving from one knowledge to another).[40]

Besides choice, St. Thomas discusses (in the course of *S.T.*, I–II) five other acts of human willing. Wishing or willing an end (*velle*, q. 10, 2) is a simple movement of approval of something good in itself, an end. Enjoyment (*fruitio*, q. 11, 4) is a resting of the will in a good that has been attained, whether imperfect or perfect; it is volitional satisfaction. Intention (*intentio*, q. 12, 1, ad 4m) is a volitional act of tending toward an end as something for which to strive. Consent (*consensus*, q. 15, 1) is a volitional act of accepting certain means as appropriate to an end under consideration. Use (*usus*, q. 16, 1) is a will-act of applying other powers of the person, or other things, in the execution of an action. Along with the act of choice, these various acts have been arranged in a systematic table of will functions which more or less summarizes this analysis.[41]

Love is also a type of will-act which St. Thomas discusses. His explanation of loving is rather complicated and it is not easy to determine how love is related to the six types of volitional activity that have just been described.[42] In general, love is the initial change or movement in an appetite that is aroused by an object of appetition.[43] It is further described as an approval or pleasure associated with an object of appetition. On the sensory level, love is attributed to the concupiscible appetite and is said to precede desire. Actually, St. Thomas uses three different terms for love. In the generic sense, love is called *amor* and seems to designate any type of appetitive approval. As a movement of will, love is called *dilectio*. Where the object of love is esteemed for its great value (*inquantum id quod amatur magni pretii aestimatur*), the word used is *caritas* (endearment).[44] Frequently *caritas* (translated as charity) signifies the love of God for His own sake, or of creatures for God's sake.[45]

Another will-act named by Aquinas is desire (*desiderium*). It is described as an appetition for something that is not yet attained.[46] On the rational level, desire is an inclination of the will toward some good that is to be sought.[47] Such volitional desire is said to flow from love; hence desire may be but another name for intention and love another name for simple willing (*velle*). The terminology fluctuates and is not clear in relation to the will-acts in the foregoing analysis.

What is clear is the fact that Thomas Aquinas has made a very profound study of volition. It is one of the most fully developed analyses that can be found in the history of Western thought. Later Scholasticism lost many of the precisions that are found in St. Thomas' writings and altered his view of will as intellectual appetite. Many so-called "Thomistic" textbooks, in the present century, offer explanations of will that are but travesties of the original. The theory of liberty of indifference does not appear in St. Thomas' works. It is possible that his explanation of the exercise of the will as something wholly undetermined by the object could be developed into an indifference theory. However, the general trend of Aquinas' explanation of volition is hard to ac-

commodate to the notion of indifference. Certainly, he did
not regard a will-act as an unmotivated activity. The point of
his teaching is that every action of will has a reason or end
to which it is directed. Motivation is not a matter of being
pushed to do something but of being attracted, in the order
of final causality, so that the intrinsic efficiency of the will
itself responds with the exercise of its power.

In the later middle ages and the early modern period,
many thinkers continue to treat the human will as a power
of rational appetition, much as St. Thomas did. Cajetan (A.D.
1469–1534) has already been mentioned for his formalization
of the analysis of will-acts.[48] It is unnecessary to repeat the
various formulations of the same view of will, as they are
found in the later Thomistic school. It might be noted that
John Buridan (fourteenth-century), whose name has been
falsely associated with the theory of liberty of indifference
because of the story of "Buridan's Ass" which is not found
in his extant works, was actually very close to Aquinas in
his understanding of will.[49] Another theologian whose psychology of human volition embraces a rational appetite
theory not unlike that of St. Thomas is John Calvin (A.D.
1509–1564).[50] He clearly distinguishes the human intellect
from the will and regards the intellect as the directive power.[51]
The distinctive feature of Calvin's view of the human will
is, of course, the contention that it is so weakened and de-
praved by the Fall of Adam that no rectitude is possible in
human willing, when man is left by God to his own devices.[52]

Of the major figures in the history of modern philosophy,
Leibniz is the best example of a thinker who adopted the
rational appetite meaning of will. He plainly teaches that
man's will is a power whose action is a tendency (*conatus,
appétition*) toward what is thought to be good and away
from what is considered evil.[53] Although he is somewhat

influenced by the intellectualist position of Spinoza, and uses his terminology (e.g. *conatus*), Leibniz clearly distinguishes cognition from volition.[54] He even maintains that willing sometimes takes place without an express judgment of the understanding.[55] He is much opposed to the view that the human will is free with a liberty of indifference, arguing that the will cannot in the concrete be presented with indifferent objects and that there must always be a sufficient reason for volitional activity.[56]

The reason why Leibniz understands volition in terms of rational appetition is his partial retention of the concept of final causality. Teleological metaphysics has not been favored by modern philosophers, apart from Leibniz, and with its disappearance has come the abandonment of appetite theories of will.

In summary, we may conclude that this appetite theory of will makes it both a power of man and a series of tendential acts. The power of will is attributed to the rational level of man's soul. Thus understood, the power of will requires the cooperation of the human intellect for its functioning. Nothing is willed that is not, in some sense, understood. Activities of willing include: wishing, intending, consenting, choosing, enjoying, using and loving. All such acts are directed to intellectually known objects or goods.

NOTES

1. Panaetius' analysis is preserved in c. 26 of the *De natura hominis* of Nemesius (ed. Matthaei, Magdeburg, 1802, p. 249; reprinted in *PG* 40). For a tabular listing of the Greek names of the various vital powers, consult: G. Verbeke, *L'Evolution de la doctrine du Pneuma, du Stoicisme à Saint Augustin* (Paris-Louvain: Desclée de Brouwer, 1945), p. 95.

2. Plotinus, *Ennaed* IV, 23 (in *Ennéades*, éd. Bréhier, Paris: Les Belles Lettres, 1927, t. IV, 90).

3. John Damascene's *Pege gnoseos* is printed in *PG* 94. The partial translation (*De fide orthodoxa*) by Burgundio has been edited as: J. Damascene, *De Fide Orthodoxa*, ed. E. M. Buytaert (St. Bonaventure, N. Y.: Franciscan Institute, 1955).

4. This passage is from Chapter 22 of Burgundio's translation, as transcribed from MS Paris, B.N. 14557, fol. 204vb–205va, by O. Lottin, in *Psychologie et morale* (Louvain-Gembloux: J. Duculot, 1942), t. I (II), 397–399; for the Greek text, *PG* 94, 944. Cf. D. Siedler, *Intellectualismus und Voluntarismus bei Albertus Magnus*, BGPM (Münster, 1941) XXXVI, 2, p. 15; and F. J. Adelmann, *The Rational Appetite in St. John Damascene* (St. Louis University Dissertation, 1955).

5. The distinction of irrational and rational appetition is more evident if we go back to Chapters 13–15, *De fide orthodoxa*, where pleasure, pain and fear are referred to sensory appetiton.

6. Nemesius, *De natura hominis*, *PG* 40, 516C–673B, has verbal parallels with Damascene's Chapters 12 to 22; some of the material in Damascene's c. 22 is very similar to Maximus, *Opuscula Theologica ad Marinum*, *PG* 91, 12C–16A. Cf. B. Domanski, *Die Psychologie des Nemesius*, BGPM III, 1–2 (Münster, 1900) pp. 129–159, for the antecedents of Nemesius.

7. Cf. E. Dobler, *Nemesius von Emesa und die Psychologie des menschlichen Aktes bei Thomas v. Aquin* (Freiburg, Switzerland: St. Paul's Press, 1950). St. Thomas cites Nemesius under the name Gregory Nyssenus.

8. Avicenna, *Liber Sextus Naturalium* (*De Anima*), Klubertanz transcription (St. Louis, *The Modern Schoolman*, 1949), pp. 19–22.

9. See A. M. Goichon, *Lexique de la langue philosophique d'Ibn Sīnā* (Paris: Desclée, 1938), p. 146 (on sensory and intellectual will) and p. 115 (on the two kinds of choice).

10. Gundissalinus, *De anima*, ed. J. T. Muckle, in *Mediaeval Studies*, II (1940), 31–103; Chapter X: *De viribus animae rationalis*, pp. 84–103. The nearest approach to a mention of *voluntas* is in the first chapter (ed. Muckle, p. 33): "Anima ergo est quae corpora animat et sensificat et voluntario motu movet." There is some discussion of this *motus voluntarius* but nowhere is it tied to a theory of rational appetition.

11. Averroes of Cordova, *Commentarium Magnum in Aristotelis De Anima Libros*, ed. F. S. Crawford (Cambridge: Medieval Academy of America, 1953); and *Compendia Librorum Aristotelis qui*

Parva Naturalia Vocantur, ed. E. L. Shields and H. Blumberg, *id.*, 1949.

12. Averroes, *Kašf ʿan Manāhiŷ*, trans. into Spanish by Manuel Alonso, S.J., in *Teologia de Averroes* (Madrid-Granada: Escuelas de Estudios Arabes, 1947), p. 326: "La voluntad no es otra cosa que un deseo motivado en nosotros como consecuencia de una imaginación o de un juicio."

13. Algazel, *Metaphysica*, ed. J. T. Muckle (Toronto: Pontifical Institute of Mediaeval Studies, 1933), p. 74 (a summary of the views of Avicenna).

14. See N. M. Haring, "Gilbert of Poitiers, Author of the 'De discretione animae, spiritus et mentis,'" *Mediaeval Studies*, XXII (1960), 174–191; see p. 171: "Whereas *sensualitas* is in the soul, the power called *voluntas* is only in the mind."

15. Hugh, *De Sacramentis*, I, 3, 21; *PL* 176, 225; cf. B. Romeyer, *La Philosophie chrétienne jusqu'à Descartes* (Paris: Bloud et Gay, 1937), III, 60.

16. For the general impact of the "new Aristotle" on the thirteenth century, consult: F. Vansteenberghen, *Aristotle in the West*, trans. L. Johnston (Louvain: Nauwelaerts, 1955).

17. P. Michaud-Quantin, "La Classification des puissances de l'âme au XIIe siècle," *Revue du Moyen-Age Latin*, V (1949), 15–34; "Albert le Grand et les puissances de l'âme," *RMAL*, XI (1955), 59–86.

18. On this development, consult: O. Lottin, "Libre arbitre et liberté depuis s. Anselme jusqu'à la fin du XIIIe siècle," in *Psychologie et morale* (1942), tome I, 11–389.

19. O. Lottin, "La Psychologie de l'acte humain chez s. Jean Damascène et les théologiens du XIIIe siècle occidental," in *Psychologie et morale*, I, 393–424.

20. Albertus Magnus, *Summa de Creaturis*, II, q. 65, 2, sol. (*Opera Omnia*, ed. Borgnet, Paris: Vivès, 1890–1899, V, 550): "Voluntas . . . stricte dicitur appetitus rationalis animae, et in hac significatione propriissime accipitur." (This work was written before A.D. 1243.)

21. *Ibid.*, II, q. 68, 1, sol. (V, 559).

22. *Ibid.*, ad quaest. (V, 560). Cf. G. Reilly, *The Psychology of St. Albert Compared with That of St. Thomas* (Washington: Catholic University Press, 1934), pp. 75–83.

23. Bonaventure, *In II Sent.*, 38, 2, 1, concl. (*Opera*, edito manualis, Quaracchi, 1938, II, 925): "triplex est appetitus, videlicet naturalis,

sensualis sive animalis, et rationalis." (This work was probably completed before A.D. 1250.)

24. *In II Sent.*, 24, 1, 2, 1, ad 2m (*ed. cit.*, II, 578). On the general relation of Bonaventure's psychology to that of Aquinas: C. M. O'Donnell, *The Psychology of St. Bonaventure and St. Thomas Aquinas* (Washington: Catholic University Press, 1937); and E. Lutz, *Die Psychologie Bonaventuras, BGPM* (Münster, 1909), VI, 4–5.

25. For more extensive interpretations: G. Verbeke, "Le développement de la vie volitive d'après saint Thomas," *Revue Philosophique de Louvain*, 56 (1958), 1–34; G. P. Klubertanz, "The Root of Freedom in St. Thomas's Later Works," *Gregorianum*, 42 (1961), 701–721, and the bibliography, pp. 722–724.

26. The Thomistic "will" must be a somewhat passive potency; otherwise it could not be a potency in which habits (such as justice and charity) could be formed. See *De virtutibus in communi*, art. 1 (for the view that virtuous habits develop only in powers that are partly active and partly passive) and art. 5 (for the view that the human will is precisely such a power). These questions on virtue date from the second Paris professorate, A.D. 1269–1272.

27. See *In Ethic.* I, lect. 1, nn. 10–11; *De veritate*, XXII, 1, c.: "appetere autem nihil aliud est, quam aliquid petere, quasi tendere in aliquid ad ipsum ordinatum."

28. On this notion of *adeptio* or *consecutio*, see: *S.T.*, I–II, 1, 8, c.; 2, 7, c.

29. *S.T.*, I. 59, 2, c.: "Similiter nec potest [voluntatem] esse idem quod intellectus angeli vel hominis. Unde ea ratione se extendit eius intellectus in id quod est extra se, secundum quod illud quod extra ipsum est per essentiam, natum est aliquo modo in eo esse: nam cognitio fit per hoc quod cognitum est in cognoscente; voluntas vero se extendit in id quod extra est, secundum quod quadam inclinatione quodammodo tendit in rem exteriorem."

30. *S.T.*, I–II, 8, 1, c.

31. Cf. R. R. Baker, *The Thomistic Theory of the Passions and Their Influence upon the Will* (Notre Dame, Ind.: University of Notre Dame Press, 1941).

32. *S.T.*, I–II, 1, 5, c. gives three arguments why there must be only one ultimate end for all men; *ibid.*, 7, c. speaks of this end as the perfect good (*bonum completissimum*) and art. 8, c. calls it God ("Deus est ultimus finis hominis et omnium aliarum rerum").

33. *S.T.*, I–II, 10, 1, c.: "Alio modo dicitur natura quaelibet substantia vel quodlibet ens."

34. *Ibid.*

35. *Ibid.*, ad primum: "Sed quia voluntas in aliqua natura fundatur, necesse est quod motus proprius naturae, quantum ad aliquid, participetur a voluntate; sicut quod est prioris causae, participatur a posteriori."

36. *Ibid.*, ad tertium.

37. *S.T.*, I–II, 10, 2, c.

38. *Ibid.*, ad tertium.

39. *S.T.*, I–II, 13, 1, c: "Sic igitur ille actus quo voluntas tendit in aliquid quod proponitur ut bonum, ex eo quod per rationem est ordinatum ad finem, materialiter quidem est voluntatis, formaliter autem rationis."

40. *S.T.*, I, 83, 4, c.

41. For an example of such an analytic table, see: V. J. Bourke, *Ethics* (New York: Macmillan, 1951), p. 64.

42. For secondary studies of St. Thomas' views on love, see *infra*, Chapter VI, note 23.

43. *S.T.*, I–II, 26, 2, c.: "Prima ergo immutatio appetitus ab appetibili vocatur amor, qui nihil est aliud quam complacentia appetibilis."

44. *S.T.*, I–II, 26, 3, c.

45. *S.T.*, II–II, 23, 1, c.; *Quaest. Disp. de Caritate*, 1, c.

46. *S.T.*, I–II, 33, 2, c. This statement is in the context of a discussion of sensory appetition but the same term, *desiderium*, is used in reference to volitional activity, for instance in *Summa contra Gentiles*, III, 26.

47. *Summa contra Gentiles*, III, 26.

48. Cajetan, *Commentarium in S.T.*, I–II, 16, 4 (the text of Cajetan is printed with the work of Aquinas, *ad loc. cit.*, in the Leonine edition).

49. Cf. E. J. Monahan, "Human Liberty and Free Will according to John Buridan," *Mediaeval Studies*, XVI (1954), 72–86.

50. For a more thorough outline of Calvin's psychology of will, see: Alexander, *Theories of Will*, pp. 142–150.

51. "Sit autem officium intellectus, inter objecta discernere, prout unumquodque probandum aut improbandum visum fuerit: voluntatis autem, eligere et sequi quod bonum intellectus dictaverit, aspernari ac fugere quod ille improbaverit." *Christianae Religionis Institutio*, I, XV, 7; cited by Alexander, p. 146.

52. "Sic voluntas quia inseparabilis est ab hominis natura, non periit: sed pravis cupiditatibus devincta fuit, ut nihil rectum appetere queat." *Ibid.*, II, II, 12.

53. G. W. Leibniz, *Mantissa Codicis Juris Gentium*, Praefatio,

(in *Philosophical Papers and Letters,* ed. L. Loemker, 2 vols. (Chicago: University of Chicago Press, 1956), I, 695).

54. See his *Refutation of Spinoza* (in *Leibniz Selections,* ed. P. Wiener, New York: Scribner, 1951, p. 495).

55. *Theodicy,* trans. E. M. Huggard (London: Routledge, 1952), p. 151.

56. *Correspondance Leibniz-Clarke,* ed. A. Robinet (Paris: Presses Universitaires, 1957), p. 129.

CHAPTER IV

Freedom as the Genus of Volition

[Speech as the Source of Volume]

MANY PEOPLE UNDERSTAND WILLING in terms of the exercise of freedom. In this view, to will means to decide or do as one pleases, without compulsion from factors internal or external to the personality of the volitional agent. Liberty or freedom thus becomes a generic notion for the definition of volition. Proponents of this approach to will frequently speak of free will and oppose any suggestion that acts of willing can be, in any sense, necessitated.

Freedom can mean many things, of course.[1] For our purposes, here, it may be described as that power or condition of an agent which enables him to act, or refuse to act, and to do so in ways which he determines, without compelling restraints from forces external to, or internal to, his own personality.[2] Actually, it is very difficult to state what freedom means, unless one first establishes a philosophical framework in terms of which it may be defined. If one calls it a "power," this could imply a faculty psychology or simply a general capacity of the agent. If one relates it to self-determination or self-perfection, this implies a theory of "self." If one defines personal freedom as the ability to do as one wills, then the issue in this chapter has been predetermined by including the notion of *willing* in the basic definition. Most of the thinkers whose views are to be considered in this chapter would agree on the following two statements: (1)

an agent is not free when he is prevented from acting, or primarily moved to act, by virtue of some forces or efficient causes outside the agent; and (2) an agent is not free when he acts in the one way that he is necessitated to act, by his own nature.

We do not find Greek philosophers of the pre-Christian period equating volition with the exercise of freedom. Plato and Aristotle do discuss human freedom but this usually occurs in the context of political or social liberty. At one point in the *Republic*, Plato argues that freedom is a factor in happiness; then he hastens to add that such freedom does not mean the license to do whatever one likes.[3] Platonic freedom is the ability to act in accord with reason and the common good. Likewise, Aristotle never suggests that the genus of willing is freedom; although some translations may suggest that he does.[4] We have already seen that neither Plato nor Aristotle has a special power of will; *boulesis*, as a sort of rational desire, is not associated, in classical Greek philosophy, with any definite theory of freedom.

The situation is somewhat different, when we come to Plotinus. He wrote and taught in the third century of the Christian era. It is possible that his teacher, Ammonius Saccas, knew something of Jewish and Christian teachings; certainly, Plotinus' pupil Porphyry did.[5] As we shall see shortly, the concept of free will is strong in the Bible and in Patristic thought. Plotinus may have been influenced by this tradition. In the opening sections of the Sixth *Ennead* there is a remarkable meditation on the relation of liberty of the person (*to eleutheron*) and willing (*boulesis*).[6] Starting from the Aristotelian notion of the *hekousion* (that which is under our control), Plotinus moves to the idea of "that which depends on us"; then he decides that "what depends on us" must be subservient to our will only.[7] Next he discusses what it means to be "master of one's action" (*tou ergou kurion*) and again decides that this reduces to will.[8] Moving on to the related notion of the free (*to eleutheron*), Plotinus wonders whether an action that is controlled by the nature of the agent can be called free. Finally, since he is a Greek, he concludes that mastery of one's own, free activity is rooted in intelligence (*nous*).[9] It is after this meditation on human freedom that Plotinus goes on to make what he calls a "daring suggestion" that there is will and freedom in the One.

This Plotinian passage approaches the view that to will is to exercise freedom. It is the closest approach to the identification of will and freedom that is to be found in non-Christian Greek speculation. St. Augustine may have known something of this text, when he wrote his treatise, *On the Free Choice of the Will*, a century later.

In the Old Testament, human thoughts, decisions and actions are said to spring from the "heart."[10] The heart is the name for the basic liberty within the human person. No distinction of special psychological powers is required. "Understanding is not separate from action. . . . Proceeding from man's heart it is the act of his inmost liberty, and cannot be distinguished from the practical dispositions of the heart that does the choosing."[11] We shall see more of this Biblical usage, concerning the heart, in Chapter Six.

This view, that each man is free in the innermost thoughts and choices of his heart, is continued in the New Testament. St. Paul emphasizes the teaching that the Christian enjoys a higher freedom, through belief in Christ.[12] This does not mean that natural freedom is denied. St. Augustine is following St. Paul, in saying: "for it is free to the extent that it has been liberated, and to that extent is it called will (*voluntas*)."[13] This statement immediately follows and helps to explain the much quoted Augustinian definition of will as "a movement of the soul, with no compulsion, toward something that is not to be given up, or that is to be attained."[14] For Augustine, will in man designates the whole soul as freely acting.[15]

St. Augustine, then, is a Patristic thinker who defines will in terms of freedom. This is very clear in a passage from one of his mature works:

Now, in us will is always free but it is not always good. For it is either free from justice, when subservient to sin, and then it is evil; or it is free from sin, when subservient to justice, and then it is good.[16]

Not only the higher freedom in which Christians share is a gift of God, according to Augustine, but also that lower freedom of will whereby man is able to pursue either good or evil.[17] God gives both free choice (*liberum arbitrium*) and freedom from sin (*libertas*) to man.[18]

This continues to be the position of most Christian teachers for many centuries. St. Anselm of Canterbury retains the Augustinian view of human will, as the free activity of the whole soul. Anselm stresses the importance of motivation: when man wills, he wills "on account of something" (*propter quod*). One may will to do something: (1) for the sake of one's own advantage; or (2) for the sake of what is right, or in accord with the will of God (which is the supreme rectitude). The first type of motivation is a disposition of the will toward what is naturally suitable (*affectio ad commodum*); the second is a disposition to the highest rectitude (*affectio justitiae*).[19] In both cases man's will is free but only the freedom under divine justice is truly meritorious.

One could also say that St. Bernard of Clairvaux taught that willing is co-extensive with all the spiritual activities of the human soul, and that the better these activities are the freer they are. The function of the will is to love; the highest love is that of divine charity; and charity makes men most free.[20] According to St. Bernard, will is the seat of man's greatest perfection. The image of God in man consists in three freedoms: (1) freedom from necessity, (2) freedom from sin, and (3) freedom from misery.[21] In its highest sense, human volition is the exercise of freedom.[22] St. Bernard's emphasis on the primacy of volitional experience in the soul's mystical union with God provides much of the stimulus for the development of psychological voluntarism in four-teenth-century Scholasticism.[23]

Franciscan theologians took a great interest in psychology, during the thirteenth and fourteenth centuries.[24] One of the characteristics of this school is a special emphasis on the spontaneity, autonomy and essential freedom of the human will. Representative of a rather extreme position within this school is Peter John Olivi who was active in the last quarter of the thirteenth century. He distinguished the human in-tellect from the human will, as did nearly all thinkers in his century. However, Olivi treated the will by appealing di-rectly to his own psychic experience.[25] His reports leave little doubt that he considered personal liberty to be identical with the will.

Most evidently [Olivi writes], we have experience within our-selves that our will restrains itself, not only from indifferent ob-jects but also from many things that it desires, restraining itself and also man's other powers. . . . We also experience how it often impels and moves itself toward things for which it has previously held repugnance and hatred, as in the case of loving one's enemy.[26]

The human will, as a self-moving potency, must be free.[27] As this point is summarized, in a recent study of Olivi, "either the free will is free, or it is not a will."[28] Even the human intellect is unable to operate unless it be applied to its work by the free will. Speculative understanding of truth depends on the volitional freedom of man.[29] All human actions are free because they stem from the will.

Olivi's position is an extreme type of psychological voluntarism which reduces the other powers of man to the status of secondary instruments. This view is related to a trend in late thirteenth-century Scholastic thinking which owes its origins, at least in part, to Bishop Etienne Tempier's condemnations (Paris, 1270 and 1277) of passive theories of will.[30] In brief, the Bishop forbade anyone to teach in his diocese that the human will is in any way subject to causal influence from the object of appetition, or from man's knowledge.[31] After this ecclesiastical act, many theologians insisted that the human will is a completely active and self-determining power, and that volitional acts are wholly caused by the will itself.[32] In other words, volition becomes more and more identified with the exercise of personal freedom.

It is in fourteenth-century Scholasticism that we find the most definite identification, by medieval thinkers, of the human will with freedom. Duns Scotus represents a transitional stage in the movement from an appetite theory of human volition to a free, efficient cause theory. Scotus explains that the will is really two "appetites," one is natural and the other is free.[33] As natural, the human will (*voluntas ut natura*) is, like any other nature, inclined to its perfective good. This natural appetite is not an *activity* of volition but is simply an inclination (*inclinatio*) toward what is good for man's intellectual nature. In Scotistic language, this natural appetite is not an elicited act.[34] He compares it to the "natural appetite" which Aristotle says matter has for form: not an activity but a proclivity.[35] Scotus admits that this first appetite in the human will is in no sense free. As free, the human will is a wholly active power of the soul, capable of acting in accord with reason or in opposition to it. It cannot act without some intellectual knowledge of its object but this cognitive presentation of the object of willing is not a cause of volition; knowledge is merely a condition of volitional activity.[36] In this second sense, of an active, operative power eliciting various actions of volition, the human will is essentially free.[37] As Scotus puts it bluntly: "nothing other than the will is the total cause of volition in the will."[38] Thus the free will is, for Scotus, a *perfect* potency capable of determining itself to act or not to act, and to accept or reject any object presented to it by the understanding.[39]

Scotus introduces the notion of "indifference" (*prima indifferentia*) to explain the initial condition of the will as it is free. The first act of understanding is not free but, once some intellectual object is presented to the will, the will is indifferent (i.e. not in any way determined) toward this object. The will may direct the intellect to consider this object or another, and the will may accept it or reject it (*velle vel nolle*).[40] Provided a man has some knowledge to start with, his will is in first act (as contrasted with second act which is the activity of volition). In first act, the will is free: a) to will or not will; b) in regard to conflicting means; and c) in regard to opposed results of its action.[41]

It is even possible that Scotus is the source, in Scholastic literature, of the much discussed story of the poor animal who is equally attracted by two piles of hay and, not being endowed with liberty of indifference, is unable to decide which way to turn. Under the guise of "Buridan's Ass," this animal has a long history in discussions of free will. Scotus has a bull who sees some grass but, just as he is turning to eat it, the bull is attracted by a more delectable object. Scotus says that this chance impediment would not be within the power of the will, even if the agent were a man instead of a bull. Then he suggests a situation in which two equally attractive objects might be presented to the agent (objective indifference). Scotus eventually says that the bull could not settle such a problem but a human will could.[42]

William of Ockham is another fourteenth-century thinker who defines will in terms of freedom. Though he reacts to, and frequently criticizes, Duns Scotus, Ockham was strongly influenced by his Franciscan predecessor. Actually, he did not distinguish the intellect and will as really different powers.[43] As a result, the earler Scholastic discussions of the relative contributions of intellect and will to human liberty lose a good deal of their meaning in the works of Ockham. However, he does differentiate between the functions of cognition and volition. In point of fact, Ockham seems to take it as unquestioned that willing is the exercise of liberty. "I call liberty," he says, "the power (*potestaem*) whereby I am able, indifferently and contingently, to put forth an effect (*effectum ponere*), in such a way that I am able to cause and not to cause the same effect, without any change being made in this power.[44] What he means when he says that the will causes "contingently," is simply this: given all the conditions required for a volitional action, the will is as able not to act, as it is to act.[45]

Ockham admits that he cannot offer demonstrative proof that free volition occurs in the human agent. This is partly because he has such a rigorous notion of demonstration that, apart from mathematics and some conclusions in logic, very little can be demonstrated. Actually, he is quite certain that man wills and does so freely, for he claims that a man directly experiences his ability to will or refuse any suggestion of reasoning.[46]

From the foregoing, one may gather that volitional activity is viewed, in Ockhamism, in the context of efficient causality. The will is said to cause or place an *effectum:* this term "effect" means the product of efficient causation, in four-teenth-century Latin. Indeed, Ockham makes efficient caus-ality the primary type and thus assists in the late medieval trend to abandon formal and final causes.[47] As a result of this, Ockham's notion of will reduces to a pure putting-forth of energy by the soul. Such an explanation approximates the meaning of a "force" in early modern physics. Obviously, it is free of restraint—unless there be a higher, or more powerful, force. In point of fact, there is such a higher (and so, freer) force: this is the Will of God.

Thus far in our examination of the meaning of will in libertarian thought of the middle ages, we have confined the investigation to questions concerning the will of man. Ac-tually much is said about the will of God, in the same literature. When volition is attributed to God, in this period, most thinkers understand the divine will in terms of their theory of human will. If they regard man's will and intellect as two cooperating powers (as Aquinas did), then they try to explain God's activity in terms of a similar duality—always with the reservation that there is no real difference in God of being, powers and activities. If they regard man's will as the soul freely producing any and all psychic activities (as Ockham did), then they see God as an infinite, omnipotent Will.[48]

The notion that will means an essentially free power con-tinues to be dominant in later Scholasticism. In mid-sixteenth century the Council of Trent defined the freedom of the

human will in terms of the power of indifference.[49] Francis
Suarez strongly supports the notion that human will is completely free, both in the choosing of means and in the intending of an end.[50] The Suarezian will is the faculty of freedom.[51]
The view of Thomas Aquinas, that will is a rational appetite
with some necessary activities and some free ones, drops out
of sight and is replaced (during the fourteenth century and
down to the present day, in most writings by Catholic philosophers and theologians) by a theory of "free will" which
is basically Scotistic.[52] Thus Berard Vogt was quite right
when he concluded a study of Duns Scotus' views with
these words:

Such, then, is the theory of liberty as outlined by Duns Scotus.
It is dominated by his high regard for the will as the queen and
mistress of man's faculties. In fact, its distinctive characteristic is
its defense of the absolute autonomy and sovereignty of the will.
In most practical details this theory does not differ essentially
from the views commonly held by the Schoolmen.[53]

The only thing that needs to be added is that practically
all of the Schoolmen are under the impression that they are
teaching Aquinas' theory of will.

Our best example in early modern philosophy of the
meaning of will under discussion in this chapter is Descartes.
The philosophy that he learned as a student at the Jesuit
College of La Flèche was Suarezian. It is no surprise, then,
to find that will, for Descartes, is the faculty of freedom.
"The will is so free in its nature," Descartes tells us, "that
it can never be constrained."[54] He equates will with freedom
of decision (*arbitrii libertas*).[55] As such, it is a direct presentation of introspective experience. Descartes is a strong
supporter of the liberty of indifference.

Such a positive faculty [the power of indifference] I have never denied to be in the will; indeed, in my opinion, it is found not only on all occasions when it determines itself to the kind of actions in which it is not borne by the weight of any reason toward one side more than toward the other; but it is even involved in all the will's other actions, so that it never determines itself without using it to the point that even when a very evident reason inclines us to a thing, though, morally speaking, it be difficult for us to do the contrary, nevertheless, speaking absolutely, we can do it.[56]

Descartes does not think that free will is best exemplified in that trivial situation in which the will is presented with equally appealing objects and finds itself able to select either one. This sort of objective indifference illustrates the lowest type of human freedom. Man's will is at its freest when it faces alternatives that are not indifferently balanced, where one is much better than the other, and the will is still able to opt for either one.[57] Descartes' freedom of will is a continuation of the voluntaristic tradition of St. Bernard, Peter Olivi, Duns Scotus and Ockham.[58]

Oddly, the British philosophers from Locke to Reid, who are such great advocates of political liberty, do not appear to understand will as the exercise of personal freedom. This is not to say that they deny personal freedom to man: this they vigorously support. However, with the gradual disappearance of the faculty theory of will (from Locke onward, in British philosophy), human liberty is dissociated from the field of volition. Locke explains this point of view very clearly:

So far as a man has power to think or not to think, to move or not to move, according to the preference or direction of his own mind, so far is a man free. Wherever any performance or forbearance are not equally in a man's power; wherever doing or not doing will not equally follow upon the preference of his mind directing it, there he is not free, though perhaps the action may be voluntary . . . liberty cannot be where there is no thought, no volition, no will; but there may be thought, there may be will, there may be volition, where there is no liberty.[59]

Locke is not too far removed from the basic notion of will which we find in Thomas Aquinas. He sees very well that voluntary activity is not co-extensive with free activity.[60]

Nor did Thomas Reid identify will and personal liberty. Like Locke, Reid placed freedom in the human person, as something closely allied to the working of practical reasoning, and he considered volition to be some sort of activity which follows after the exercise of freedom. As we shall see in the next chapter, Reid considers will to be a sort of executive capacity under the direction of a prior power of freedom.

Modern German philosophy provides many variations of the identification of will with freedom. Leibniz is the last of the noted German thinkers to retain something of the Thomistic notion of will. In one place he says:

The highest perfection of man consists not merely in that he acts freely but still more in that he acts with reason. Better, these are both the same thing, for the less anyone's use of reason is disturbed by the impulsion of the affections, the freer one is. . . . For freedom is the same as spontaneity with reason, and to will is to be brought to act through a reason perceived by the intellect.[61]

So Leibniz does not say that will is a power freely to will anything, whether it is reasonable or not.

It is with Kant that the first signs of will as freedom are found in German thought. He uses two words for will. The first (*der Wille*) is almost identical with practical reason; it is to be examined later, in our Chapter Eight. The second Kantian term for will (*die Willkür*) is often translated as "elective will"; it is the power of free choice.[62] In his *Introduction to the Metaphysic of Morals*, Kant states that, "only the *elective will* can be called *free*."[63] However, Kant's positive meaning of freedom is identified with the autonomy of the will, with the capacity of the rational will to legislate the directives which form a basis for moral activity.[64] The practical writings of Kant might suggest, then, that he would use freedom as a genus in terms of which he could define will.

Yet, Kant also speaks of a "will" which is not free: this is precisely the case when the elective will is subject to the sway of sensuous impulses or instincts.[65] The fact of the matter is that Kant's notions on freedom admit of a variety of interpretations and it is impossible to establish a univocal meaning for "will" in Kant.[66] The safest conclusion is to say that Kant certainly stimulated some of his followers to move in the direction of an identification of volition and the exercise of freedom.

This is the direction that J. G. Fichte followed. He regarded will as free self-determination.

My will is mine, and it is the only thing that is wholly mine and entirely dependent on myself; and through it I have already become a citizen of the realm of freedom and pure spiritual activity. What determination of my will . . . is best adapted to the order of the spiritual world is proclaimed to me at every moment by my conscience, the bond that constantly unites me to the spiritual world; it depends solely on myself to give my activity the appointed direction.[67]

With Fichte, free activity and volitional activity become coextensive. "The free being with absolute freedom, proposes to itself certain ends. It wills because it wills, and the willing of an object is itself the last ground of such willing."[68] Such an identification of will and freedom ultimately makes volition into a blind putting forth of energy: a theory with which our next chapter is to deal.

This same point of view could be illustrated in the writings of many Post-Kantians. It may even be found in Hegel, when he says:

> The Will is free only when it does not will anything alien, extrinsic, foreign to itself (for as long as it does so, it is dependent), but wills itself alone—wills the Will. This is the absolute Will—the volition to be free.[69]

It is with Schopenhauer that this voluntaristic tendency in German thought reaches a climax and breaks like a bubble. In a great *tour de force*, his *Prize Essay* first shows that free will is utterly impossible, in the phenomenal order.[70] The first four sections of the *Essay* (nine tenths of the whole work) argue that every event requires a cause, that all activities are thus governed by strict necessity, that it is only human ignorance of the total causality behind man's actions which has led theologians and philosophers to postulate freedom of will. In the course of this forceful argument, Schopenhauer displays immense historical erudition, roaming through the writings of the ancient philosophers, Greek and Latin Fathers of the Church, medieval Scholastics, and of course modern religious and philosophic writers. His repeated axiom is: *quidquid fit necessario fit* (everything happens necessarily).[71] He ridicules the whole notion of "liberty of indifference," sarcastically accusing the supporters of this view of basic ignorance.

They declare the freedom of the will to be immediately given in the self-consciousness and therefore so unshakably established that all arguments against it could be nothing but sophisms. This exalted confidence stems only from the fact that the good fellows don't even know what freedom of the will is and means, and in their innocence understand by it no more than the mastery of the will over the parts of the body, which we analyzed in the second section.[72]

If this critique of his predecessors were all that is found in the *Prize Essay*, Schopenhauer would not deserve mention in this chapter. In the final section of the *Essay*, he turns to a resounding defense of the *transcendental* freedom of man. Man is not free in his actions but he is completely free in his *esse*, in the innermost depths of his being![73] The unavoidable feeling of moral responsibility is the ground of Schopenhauer's argument for this higher freedom. Personal guilt is attributable to the character of man. And, "character is the empirically recognized, persistent, and unchangeable nature of an individual will."[74] So, in the last analysis, Schopenhauer does belong with those thinkers who identify will and freedom. He does not equate man's activities with freedom; these belong in the phenomenal order. He asks his reader to rise above this area of appearances and thus to see that, "the will is of course free, but only in itself and outside of appearance."[75]

In the course of his criticism, Schopenhauer makes a slighting reference to Maine de Biran as a fanatical supporter of the liberty of indifference approach to will.[76] Actually, this French amateur in philosophy held a theory of will that was not too far removed from Schopenhauer's. Starting from the Cartesian *Cogito*, Maine de Biran stressed the spiritual freedom of the self.

I will, I act (*cogito*), therefore I am (*ergo sum*). I am not in some indeterminate way a thinking being, but very precisely a willing force which passes from the virtual to the actual by its own energy, by determining itself or bringing itself to action.[77]

The human will is the "free force which is the essence of the soul or spirit of man."[78] It is obvious that Schopenhauer might regard de Biran's will as an offense against the principle of causality; yet they are in basic agreement on the metaphysical character of will. We shall see more on this will-metaphysics in Chapter Nine.

The association of will with an inner freedom of the self continues to be a dominant theme in the French *philosophie de l'esprit*. Renouvier, Fouillé, even Bergson, think of volition in terms of free self-determination.[79] As Gabriel Marcel says, "there is a freedom which is not concerned with doing. . . . To want, indeed,—I take this word in the sense of the French *vouloir*—is not to desire."[80] When the French existentialists speak of will, they do not mean anything like rational appetite but rather some sort of free, self-constituting reality.

This way of understanding will, as personal freedom or its exercise, is not typical of American philosophy. Adler professes to find something like this approach in John Dewey and Paul Weiss.[81] It is more obvious in the recent thinking of John Wild which shows the influence of European existentialism.[82]

The meaning of will that we have examined in this chapter reduces will to some sort of freedom. This is positive freedom, a liberty within the person to do or be what he pleases. It is close to the notion of self-determination. Such freedom is but remotely related to the absence of external restraint which is that negative view of liberty which is usually taken by people who discuss political and social freedoms. Perhaps most thinkers in the history of Western theology and philosophy who have undertaken to defend the concept of "free will" have understood will in the sense that has been described in the present chapter.

NOTES

1. Mortimer Adler concludes that there are five distinct meanings of freedom, in Western thought: (1) circumstantial freedom of self-realization, (2) acquired freedom of self-perfection, (3) natural freedom of self-determination, (4) political liberty, and (5) collective freedom. See: *Idea of Freedom* (New York: Doubleday, 1961), II, 5–11.

2. Compare Adler's general conclusion: "To be free is to have an ability or power to act in a certain way and for a certain result. To be free is, through the exercise of such power, to have what one does proceed from oneself rather than from another." *Idea of Freedom*, I, 615.

3. *Republic*, IX, 577; see Cornford's comment in *The Republic of Plato*, p. 301.

4. Thus, Aristotle, *Metaphysics*, IX, 5, 1048a10-11 (in McKeon, *Basic Works of Aristotle*, p. 825) reads in the Oxford translation: "There must, then, be something else that decides; I mean by this, desire or will." Actually, the last word should have been translated "choice" (*proairesis*).

5. Cf. J. Daniélou, *Origen*, trans. W. Mitchell (New York: Sheed & Ward, 1955), pp. 76–77.

6. Plotinus, *Ennead* VI, 8, 1–6 (ed. Bréhier, t. VI, 2, pp. 134–140).

7. *Ibid.*, VI, 8, 1, p. 134 (Greek text, lines 30–32).

8. *Ibid.*, 2–3, pp. 135–136.

9. *Ibid.*, 4–5, pp. 137–138.

10. Cf. C. Tresmontant, *A Study of Hebrew Thought* (New York: Desclée Co., 1960); Part Three: Understanding, ch. 1, The Heart of Man, pp. 117–124; and ch. 2, Mind and Action, pp. 125–131.

11. *Ibid.*, p. 127.

12. See Gal. 5:13: "For you have been called to liberty, brethren; only do not use liberty as an occasion for sensuality." Cf. W. F.

Lynch, "The Problem of Freedom," *Cross Currents*, X (1960), 98–101, for a discussion of further texts in St. Paul.

13. St. Augustine, *Retractationes*, I, 15, 4: "In tantum enim libera est, in quantum liberata est, et in tantum apellatur voluntas."

14. *Ibid.*, I, 15, 3: "Quae voluntas utique, sicut definita est, animi motus fuit, nullo cogente, ad aliquid vel non amittendum vel adipiscendum."

15. The whole force of Augustine's trinitarian psychology (*De Trinitate*, X, in toto) is that the whole human soul can be called either *mens*, *memoria* or *voluntas*. As acting or doing, the whole soul is will; there is no faculty psychology in Augustine.

16. St. Augustine, *De gratia et libero arbitrio*, 15, 31: "Semper est autem in nobis voluntas libera, sed non semper est bona."

17. St. Augustine, *De libero arbitrio*, II, 1; *De civitate Dei*, V, 9–10.

18. *De civitate Dei*, XXII, 30.

19. St. Anselm, *De concordia praescientiae Dei cum libero arbitrio*, III, 11–13; *PL* 158, 534–540. Cf. J. R. Sheets, "Justice in the Moral Thought of St. Augustine," *The Modern Schoolman*, XXV (1948), 132–139; I. Choquette, "Voluntas, affectio and potestas in Anselm," *Mediaeval Studies*, IV (1942), 61–81.

20. St. Bernard, *De diligendo Deo*, 12 (in the trans. by A. C. Pegis, in *Wisdom of Catholicism*, New York: Random House, 1949, p. 262).

21. St. Bernard, *De gratia et libero arbitrio*, 3–5; *PL* 182, 1007–1010.

22. Cf. A. Forest, F. Van Steenberghen, M. de Gandillac, *Le Mouvement doctrinal du IXe au XIVe siècle* (Paris: Bloud et Gay, 1951), pp. 128–131.

23. On the extension of will into the area of cognitive functions, in St. Bernard and William of St. Thierry, see: E. Gilson, *La Théologie mystique de s. Bernard* (Paris: Vrin, 1934), pp. 226–228. For the fourteenth-century influence, K. Michalski, "Le problème de la volonté à Oxford," *Studia Philosophica*, II (1937), 261.

24. William of Vaurouillon, O.F.M., a Scotist author of the fifteenth century, incorporates a good deal of this Franciscan psychology into his *Liber de Anima*. See the edition by I. Brady, in *Mediaeval Studies*, X (1948), 225–297; XI (1949), 247–307.

25. E. Bettoni, "La libertà come fondamento dei valori umani nel pensiero di Pier di Giovanni Olivi," in *Atti del XII Congresso Int. di Filosofia* (Firenze, 1960) XI, 39–47.

26. Peter John Olivi, *Quaestiones in II librum Sententiarum*, q. 57 (Quaracchi: Bibliotheca Franciscana Scholastica, 1922–1926), vol.

II, 325: "Certissime enim intra nos experimur quod voluntas nostra retinet se non solum ab indifferentibus, etc."

27. *Ibid.*, II, 329: "Ergo oportet voluntatem, prout est potentia sui ipsius motivam, esse liberam."

28. "O la volontà è libera, o non è volontà." Bettoni, *art. cit.*, p. 45.

29. "Videtur mihi quod intellectus ex eo quod est unitus voluntati sortitur tam in modo existendi quam in modo aspiciendi objecta sua quidam sublimitatem et quoddam regimen sine quo non posset, saltem ita alte, veritatem speculari." Olivi, quaest. 57, *id.*, II, 331. Earlier (II, 323), Olivi remarks: "Certum est autem quod intellectus non movetur tunc nec tenetur nisi a voluntate nostra."

30. For the text of Tempier's condemnations of 1277, which touch on certain teachings of Thomas Aquinas, see: *Fontes Vitae S. Thomae Aquinatis*, ed. M. H. Laurent (Saint Maximin: *Revue Thomiste*, 1937), VI, 596–614. In so far as they applied to St. Thomas, these condemnations were revoked in Paris, by Bishop Etienne Bourret, in A.D. 1325. *Ibid.*, VI, 666–667.

31. A. J. Denomy, "The *De Amore* of Andreas Capellanus and the Condemnation of 1277," *Mediaeval Studies*, VIII (1946), 107–123, lists the theses that are concerned with *voluntas*.

32. Walter of Bruges, Gonsalvus Hispanus and William of Ware represent this movement to make will superior to intellect and absolutely free in all its actions. For details, see: A. San Cristobal-Sebastian, *Controversias acerca de la voluntad desde 1270–1300* (Madrid: Editorial y Libreria Co. Cul., 1958).

33. J. Duns Scotus, *Opus Oxoniense*, IV, d. 49, q. 10, n. 2 (*Opera*, ed. L. Wadding, Paris: Vivès, 1891–1895, t. XXI, 318): "Duplex est appetitus in voluntate, scilicet naturalis et liber." The same point is more fully explained by Scotus in *Reportata Parisiensia*, IV, 49, 9, nn. 3–5 (ed. Wadding, XXIV, 659).

34. *Op. Ox.*, II, 39, 2: "Voluntas naturalis ut necessario tendit in volitum non habet actum elicitum circa illud, sed ipsa est tantum inclinatio quaedam in tali natura ad perfectionem sibi maxime convenientem."

35. The reference to the appetite of matter for form is in the text of *Rep. Paris.*, cited above in note 33.

36. "Sicut voluntas non potest habere actum circa ignotum, ita non potest habere actum circa obiectum sub ratione formali aliqua obiecti quae ratio est penitus ignota." *Op. Ox.*, I, 3, q. 3 (ed. Garcia, Quaracchi: Collegium S. Bonaventurae, 1912, I, 348). "Unde esto quod phantasiatio vel obiectum apprehensum requiratur ad hoc quod

sit volitio, non tamen requiritur nisi sicut causa sine qua non." *Op. Ox.*, II, 25, 1, 1, n. 19 (ed. Garcia, II, 698).

37. Scotus speaks of *voluntas* as a "potentia libera per essentiam," in the *Ordinatio*, I, 17, pars 1, qq. 1–2 (*Opera*, ed. C. Balic, Civitas Vaticana: Typis Polyglottis, 1950 ff., t. V, 169). On the question of Scotus' voluntarism, see: J. Pieper, *Scholasticism*, (New York: Pantheon Books, 1960), pp. 141–142.

38. "Dico ergo ad quaestionem, quod nihil aliud a voluntate est causa totalis volitionis in voluntate." *Op. Ox.*, II, 25, q. 1, n. 766 (ed. Garcia, II, 701).

39. On this *perfecta potentia contradictionis*, *ibid.*, n. 768d (ed. Garcia, II, 704). Scotus concludes: "Potentia igitur rationalis perfecta, cujusmodi est voluntas, quamvis sit contradictorium, poterit determinare se, objecto praesente, ad unum illorum."

40. "Prima intellectio non est in potestate nostra, sed prima indifferentia, quia potest quis se determinare ad volendum vel non volendum, hoc est a voluntate non ab intellectu, quia intellectus ab objecto naturaliter movetur . . . Sed habita prima intellectione, in potestate ejus est convertere intellectum ad considerandum hoc vel illud, et hoc vel illud velle vel nolle." *Quaestiones Quodlibetales*, XXI, n. 14 (ed. Vivès, t. XXVI); cf. *Op. Ox.*, I, d. 1, q. 4, n. 3 (ed. Vivès, VIII, 157).

41. "Voluntas in quantum est actus primus libera est: a) ad oppositos actus; b) libera etiam est mediantibus illis actibus oppositis ad opposita objecta in quae tendit; c) et ulterius ad oppositos effectus quos producit." *Op. Ox.*, I, d. 39, q. 1, a. 3.

42. *Op. Ox.*, II, d. 25, q. 1, n. 690d-e (ed. Garcia, II, 690–691). For a sympathetic exposition of Scotus' theory of free will, see: B. Vogt, "The Metaphysics of Human Liberty in Duns Scotus," *Proceedings of the American Catholic Philosophical Association* XVI (1940), 27–37.

43. "Intellectus et voluntas sunt idem realiter in se et cum essentia animae." Guillelmi Ockhami, *Super Quatuor Libros Sententiarum Subtilissimae Quaestiones*, Lib. II, 2 K (ed. Lyons, 1495).

44. *Quodlibeta Septem*, I, q. 16 (ed. Argentina, 1491); the text is cited in P. Boehner, "Ockham's Tractatus de Praedestinatione et de Praescientia Dei," *Proc. Amer. Cath. Philos. Assoc.* XVI (1940), 181, footnote 8.

45. "Praeter istos modos adhuc est unus modus, quo potest voluntas creata cessare ab actu causandi, scilicet se sola, quantumcumque nullum praedictorum desit, sed omnia sit posita, et hoc est et non aliud voluntatem contingenter causare." *Super I Sent.*, d. 38, q. 1 G.

46. *Quodl.*, I, q. 16; for the text, see Boehner, *art. cit.*, pp. 182–183, footnote 10.

47. On causality in Ockham, see Gilson's analysis of *Quodlibets* II, IV and VI, plus *Super I Sent.* d. 2, in *History of Christian Philosophy in the Middle Ages*, p. 789.

48. A. C. Pegis, "Necessity and Liberty," *Proc. Amer. Cath. Philos. Assoc.* XVI (1940), 1–27, compares Aquinas and Ockham on the matter of divine freedom.

49. Denziger-Bannwart-Umberg, *Enchiridion Symbolorum*, Romae, 1937, nn. 814–815.

50. F. Suarez, *Disputationes Metaphysicae*, disp. XIX, 8, nn. 19–20: "Libertatem voluntatis evidentius et perfectius exerceri in electione mediorum . . . ad intentionem finis fertur voluntas et sola aliqua inclinatione naturali, quamvis libere feratur." See *ibid.*, XIX, 7, n. 8.

51. T. V. Mullaney, *Suarez on Human Freedom* (Baltimore: The Carroll Press, 1950), offers a full study of Suarez' views on will and freedom; for a shorter but accurate treatment, see: T. E. Davitt, *The Nature of Law* (St. Louis: Herder, 1951), pp. 86–94.

52. See the definition of "free will" in B. Wuellner, *Dictionary of Scholastic Philosophy* (Milwaukee: Bruce, 1956), p. 49.

53. B. Vogt, *art. cit.*, p. 37.

54. R. Descartes, *Les Passions de l'âme*, I, art. 41 (ed. Adam-Tannery, Paris: Cerf, 1904, t. IX): "La volonté est tellement libre de sa nature, qu'elle ne peut jamais être contrainte."

55. *Meditationes*, IV (ed. G. Lewis, Paris: Vrin, 1946, p. 57): "Sola est voluntas, sive arbitrii libertas, quam tantam in me experior, ut nullius majoris ideam apprehendam. . . ."

56. *Lettre à Mersenne*, (ed. Adam-Tannery, III, 379). The text is cited in English, in Adler, *Idea of Freedom*, I, 524, and Adler notes the similarity to the views of Duns Scotus.

57. *Meditationes*, IV (ed. Lewis, pp. 57–58).

58. See the remarks of R. Allers, "Bemerkungen zur Anthropologie und Willenslehre des Descartes," in *Cartesio* (Milano: Società Ed. Vita e Pensiero, 1937), p. 7.

59. J. Locke, *An Essay Concerning Human Understanding*, XXI, 8.

60. J. Rickaby, *Free Will and Four English Philosophers* (London: Burns and Oates, 1906), pp. 75–111, does not correctly interpret Locke.

61. G. Leibniz, *Philosophical Papers*, "Thoughts on the Principles of Descartes," ed. L. E. Loemker (Chicago: University of Chicago Press, 1956), p. 639.

62. I. Kant, *Introduction to the Metaphysic of Morals*, in T. K.

Abbott, *Kant's Critique of Practical Reason and Other Works*, 6th ed. (London: Longmans, 1948), pp. 265–270.

63. *Ibid.*, p. 282; cf. Adler, *Idea of Freedom*, I, 526–527.

64. *Critique of Practical Reason*, trans. Abbott, p. 137.

65. *Critique of Pure Reason*, Transcendental Doctrine of Method, chap. 2, sect. 1; the point is well brought out in the translation by J. M. D. Meiklejohn (New York: Willey Book Co., 1900), p. 450.

66. For a quick sketch of the interpretations by Jones, Vaihinger and Herman Cohen, see: J. R. Rosenberg, "Freedom in the Philosophy of Kant," *Philosophical Studies in Honor of Ignatius Smith*, ed. J. K. Ryan (Westminster: Newman, 1952), 257–269.

67. From Johann Gottlieb Fichte, *The Vocation of Man*, edited with an Introduction by Roderick M. Chisholm, copyright © by The Liberal Arts Press, Inc., reprinted by the Liberal Arts Press Division of The Bobbs-Merrill Company, Inc. (New York, 1956), p. 119.

68. Fichte, *Science of Rights*, trans. A. E. Kroeger (London: Trubner and Co., 1889), p. 193.

69. G. W. F. Hegel, *Philosophy of History*, trans. J. Sibree (New York: Willey Book Co., 1900), p. 442.

70. A. Schopenhauer, *Preisschrift über die Freiheit des Willens* (1839); translated by K. Kolenda as *Essay on the Freedom of the Will* (New York: Liberal Arts Press), 1960.

71. *Ibid.*, p. 62.

72. *Ibid.*, p. 86.

73. *Ibid.*, pp. 91–99.

74. *Ibid.*, p. 95.

75. *Ibid.*, p. 97.

76. *Ibid.*, p. 86.

77. Maine de Biran, *Nouveaux essais d'anthropologie*, in *Oeuvres*, ed. Tisserand (Paris: Alcan, 1920–1949), t. XIV, pp. 318–367; the quotation is from p. 275.

78. *Ibid.*, p. 333.

79. For a survey of the self-determination theories (most of which are more or less connected with the view of will outlined in this chapter) and for many references to the French school, see Adler, *Idea of Freedom*, I, 400–545.

80. G. Marcel, *The Mystery of Being* (Chicago: Regnery, 1951), p. 110.

81. *Idea of Freedom*, I, 508–511 and 515–517.

82. J. Wild, *Human Freedom and Social Order* (Durham: Duke University Press, 1959), pp. 170 and 224.

CHAPTER V

Will as Dynamic Power

A FOURTH MEANING OF WILL identifies it with dynamic power. People who talk about training the will, or developing and increasing one's "will power," usually think of it in this way. If the appetite theory of will emphasizes the final causality of human experience, then this dynamic power view stresses the analysis of the same experience in terms of efficient causality. To will is to do or produce something. At times, this usage almost equates will with *force*, in the generalized sense of the capacity to do work.

The dynamic meaning of will is not very prominent before the Renaissance, though there may be anticipations of it in the treatment of will as a sort of spiritual energy by some Christian writers on asceticism and the spiritual life. Modern philosophers and psychologists have frequently understood and used will in this dynamic way. This is true of many British and German writers. We shall see a special form of this usage, in the "executive will" of the American Faculty Psychologists.

The relation between freedom theories of will and dynamic power theories is often very close. In fact, many of the same thinkers whose views appeared in the preceding chapter are to be examined in this chapter. However, the two usages are not identical. A man may think that the genus to which will belongs is freedom, without thinking that will means a dynamic force; and conversely, he may think of will as productive of activity, without any claim that this dynamism is free. Actually, the dynamic power notion of volition takes many variations: of which the main two are differentiated by a distinction of the end product of such a power. Frankly, some people have thought of will as the capacity to accomplish incorporeal, mental or spiritual activities, while others have used the term to designate the source of physical, corporeal or organic activities.

Most of the ancient Greek philosophers postulated a motor power in man, to which they attributed the bodily movements of the human organism, and this kinetic power is not identified with will (*boulesis*). This is obviously the case in Aristotle and his school. Plotinus is thinking of an Aristotelian division of psychic powers, when he lists the kinetic power (*ten kinesin*) as something distinct from appetition.[1] There is a sense in which Plotinus spoke of a general energy (*koinon ergon*) of the vital organism but he did not call this will.[2] The Stoics thought of the *pneuma* (vital spirit) as the efficient cause of organic functions and movements; this is especially so in the case of Chrysippus.[3] However, there is no effort to identify the *pneuma* with will.

It is possible that the many Biblical references to the Will of God, and the association of divine volition with omnipotence, may have influenced Patristic writers to use will in the sense of spiritual strength and power. In the Latin version of the Lord's Prayer, the petition "Thy will be done" (*fiat voluntas tua*) associates the divine will with the passive form of the verb "to do or make" (*facere*).[4]

We have seen, in the preceding chapter, how St. Augustine equates will in man with the whole soul as active. In the *City of God*, he explains how all of man's feelings, desires, tendencies and loves are rooted in will.[5] But there is a passage in one of Augustine's early works, in which he suggests that both the motions in man's soul and in his body are produced by willing.

He who perceives that there is will within him, perceives that the soul is moved by itself. For, if we will it is not someone else who wills for us. And this movement of the soul is spontaneous, for this has been granted it by God; yet this movement is not from place to place, as in the case of the body. And, although the soul moves its body locally by means of will, that is, by that movement which is not local, this does not show that the soul is moved locally.[6]

It is probable, then, that St. Augustine thought of human will as a strength in the soul whereby all of man's activities may be produced. In another place, he remarks:

True it is, virtue is commonly associated with the soul, and strength (*vis*) with the body. Still, I would never divorce strength from the soul, noting, as I do, that in bodies without souls no strength is present. It is through the body, of course, that the soul uses its strength, as it does the senses; however, since these are functions of a living thing, who can doubt that both belong eminently to the soul?[7]

Since Augustinian psychology is well known throughout the middle ages, and accepted by most Christian spiritual writers in this whole period, it is not too much to say that in medieval Latin usage the will of man is considered to be the soul as the seat of human activities. It is in this tradition that we find Richard Fishacre, at Oxford in the early thirteenth century, explaining that both nature and will are efficient causes within the human soul. Of the two agents, will is the more powerful and active, according to Fishacre.[8] It seems to have been characteristic of British thinkers, even in the middle ages, to emphasize the dynamic nature of will. Thomas Bradwardine (in the fourteenth century) carries the emphasis on the efficient power of will into the discussion of God's power. "The divine will," Bradwardine maintains, "is the efficient cause of each and every thing that is done [in the universe], being the mover or motor of every motion."[9] As a result of his stress on the omnipotence of the divine will, Bradwardine reduces human volition to the status of an inefficacious velleity.[10]

At the beginning of the modern period in British philosophy, Francis Bacon describes six faculties of the soul (*facultates animae*): will, intellect, reason, phantasy, memory and appetite.[11] Completely divorced from the area of appetition, the function of the Baconian will is to act. Thomas Hobbes does away with final causality: "A final cause has no place but in such things as have sense and will; and this also I shall prove hereafter to be an efficient cause."[12] His much quoted definition of will, as the last appetite in deliberating, that which puts an end to the free process of deliberation, must be understood in this context.[13] This appetite is not an inclination but an action wholly caused and necessitated by its antecedents. Thus he turns willing into the power of doing what one wills.

Neither is the freedom of willing or not willing greater in man than in other living creatures. For where there is appetite, the entire cause of the appetite hath preceded; and consequently, the act of appetite could not choose but follow, that is, hath of necessity followed. And therefore such a liberty as is free from necessity, is not to be found in the will either of men or beasts. But if by liberty we understand the faculty or power, not of willing, but of doing what they will, then certainly that liberty is to be allowed to both, and both may equally have it, whensoever it is to be had.[14]

If we recall that, "all mutation or alteration is motion or endeavour (and endeavour also is motion) in the internal parts of the thing that is altered,"[15] then it becomes clear that will, for Hobbes, is merely one type of physical force. There can be no human appetition without motion.

George Berkeley carries on the British tradition by strongly rejecting all distinctions of faculties.[16] Man is a spirit and, as Berkeley sees it: "A spirit is one simple, undivided, active being—as it perceives ideas it is called the *understanding*, and as it produces or otherwise operates about them it is called the *will*."[17] In other words, Berkeley has a dynamic power theory of will, with the following modifications: the "power" is simply the spirit itself; and what is produced is a spiritual result, never a physical event.

With David Hume the meaning of will takes a different direction. Berkeley had thrown out the various powers of man; Hume rejected the whole concept of self, or spirit. For Hume, the world including man is but a series of discrete events, of either a mental or a bodily character. This phenomenalism[18] left very little room for human volition. What Hume did was to go back to a suggestion that Locke had offered, to the effect that human desire is a vague feeling of uneasiness which the mind experiences in the absence of some good.[19] Hume decided to call will, "the internal impression we feel and are conscious of, when we knowingly give rise to any new motion of our body, or new perception of our mind."[20] The dynamic power concept of will is not, strictly speaking, maintained by Hume, for he attributes human activity (and the conscious omission of activity) to what he calls the "liberty of spontaneity." This latter is described as the "power of acting or not acting, according to the determinations of the will."[21] It is to be observed that Hume is almost forced, at times, to talk about "powers" in his analysis of human experience; however, this does not imply the existence of a real self, or of really distinguished faculties in the human person. Will is simply an affective impression, or determination, which is necessarily connected with a consequent bodily or mental activity of man. As we shall see later (Chapter Six), Hume also speaks of "heart" or "taste" as sentiments which serve as "springs" or impulses to volition and to action. It is within the dynamism of the production of human activities that the Humean will functions as an act of decision or determination, preceded by more primitive feelings of the heart and followed by other mental or bodily activities. The laws of association are simply statements of the necessary sequence of these series of events.[22]

John Stuart Mill also describes will as a moment in that series of associations which terminates in the bodily activity of man. Volition is experienced as an antecedent and bodily action as a consequent—but there is no direct consciousness that the former efficiently causes or produces the latter.[23] It is evident, then, that the early British Associationists seem convinced that other people understand the human will as a dynamic power but the Associationists are concerned to show that there is no causality, in the traditional sense, in the volition-action sequence.

Thomas Reid is the British philosopher who has most influenced common English usage in regard to volition and will. His meaning is close to that which is found, even today, in ordinary dictionaries. Reid distinguishes between "active powers" (capacties to produce directed thoughts and bodily movements) and will (the power to determine the use, or non-use, of these active powers).

Every man is conscious of a power to determine, in things which he conceives to depend upon his determination. To this power we give the name of *Will;* and, as it is usual, in the operations of the mind, to give the same name to the power and to the act of that power, the term *will* is often put to signify the act of determining, which more properly is called *volition.* Volition, therefore, signifies the act of willing and determining, and Will is put indifferently to signify either the power of willing or the act.[24]

If the general trend, then, in later British philosophy was to divorce the dynamic power of action from the prior determination of will, an opposite development may be discerned in German philosophy. Although Kant thinks of will as "a kind of causality belonging to living beings in so far as they are rational,"[25] and even as an efficient cause, it is clear that he is far from saying that will is simply a dynamic force. However, Post-Kantian philosophy moves toward the identification of will and the efficient causing of activity. Schelling emphasizes this meaning of will: "Now it is undoubtedly a *productive* activity that displays itself in volition; all free action is productive and productive only with consciousness."[26]

Running through Fichte's long-winded accounts of will as the first principle of all reality (on which see Chapter Nine) is the basic conviction that will always means a dynamic power. This meaning attaches to will, when taken in a political or collective sense by Fichte, but it is most obvious when he is talking about his personal will.

My will stands alone, apart from all that is not itself, and is its own world merely by itself and for itself; not only as being itself an absolutely *first,* primary and original power, before which there is no preceding influence by which it may be governed, but also as being followed by no conceivable or comprehensible *second* step in the series, by which its activity may be brought under the dominion of a foreign law.[27]

This same conviction that will is dynamic energy, in fact the power which moves and produces all things, is shared by Schopenhauer. He insists that the same will which his reader has come to understand in the abstract as the fundamental metaphysical principle of all reality is also concretely experienced as the only energy or force that is operative in the world of appearances.

He will recognize [Schopenhauer asserts] this will of which we are speaking not only in those phenomenal existences which exactly resemble his own, in men and animals as their inmost nature, but the course of reflection will lead him to recognize the force which germinates and vegetates in the plant, and indeed the force through which the crystal is formed, that by which the magnet turns to the north pole, the force whose shock he experiences from the contact of two different kinds of metals, the force which appears in the elective affinities of matter as repulsion and attraction, decomposition and combination, and, lastly, even gravitation, which acts so powerfully throughout matter, draws the stone to the earth and the earth to the sun,—all these, I say, he will recognize as different only in their phenomenal existence, but in their inner nature as identical, as that which is directly known to him so intimately and so much better than anything else, and which in its most distinct manifestation is called *will.*[28]

The foregoing is a rather long sentence in which Schopenhauer says that will is the dynamic power which does everything.

The same identification of *Wille* and *Macht* is, of course, made by Nietzsche. His general axiom is that will is active power. This is the way that he states his view, in *Beyond Good and Evil*:

Granted, finally, that we succeeded in explaining our entire in-stinctive life and the development and ramification of one funda-mental form of will—namely, the Will to Power, as my thesis puts it; granted that all organic functions could be traced back to this Will to Power, and that the solution of the problem of generation and nutrition—it is one problem—could also be found therein: one would thus have acquired the right to define *all* ac-tive force unequivocally as Will to Power. The world seen from the inside, the world defined and designated according to its "intelligible character"—it would simply be "Will to Power" and nothing else.[29]

This almost unbelieveable assumption that will is the one active force which produces all psychic and physical events is one of the dominant themes in nineteenth-century German philosophy. However, such a sweeping assertion does not go unchallenged. Hermann Lotze, a medical doctor turned psy-chologist and philosopher, denied that will has any direct causality in the order of bodily events. He turned back to the psycho-physical parallelism of the Post-Cartesians. For Lotze, there can be no interaction between the soul and the body of man.[30] He thinks of will as an active power but its results are purely psychic: "the will is nothing else than living voli-tion."[31] After denying that the human will moves the body, Lotze says:

Our view does not threaten the living energy of the will, or even the fact of its power over the limbs . . . as little as our will directly extends beyond the limits of our body and by its own efficiency produces changes in the distant outer world, so little does it in itself extend to more in our personality than the soul; if, nevertheless, it exerts a power over the body, which Nature has associated with it as its instrument, it is because the same necessity of Nature has ordained that its behests, in themselves powerless, be followed by an obedience of the masses under the regulation of law.[32]

The fact that Lotze feels it necessary to protest so much against the idea that the will moves the parts of man's body shows how widespread was the contrary view of will in nineteenth-century Germany.

From the end of the eighteenth century and on through the nineteenth century, a quite different meaning was given to will by the members of the school of Faculty Psychologists in the United States.[33] Though chiefly a movement in Protestant theology, in reaction to the views of Jonathan Edwards, the American Faculty Psychology has not, perhaps, received the attention that it merits in general histories of philosophy. One of the basic tenets of the school was the attribution of human functions to three powers or faculties. The first was called perception, understanding, or the power of thought: it was the knowing faculty. The second was called sensibility, affection, heart, or taste: it was the faculty of feeling, of suffering agreeable or disagreeable emotions. The third was named will or the power of volition: it was the faculty of action.

Like all philosophers who have used the word "faculty," these people had trouble with opponents or critics who thought that they meant to postulate three different agencies within man. But as President Jeremiah Day, of Yale, patiently explained it:

They are different powers of one and the same agent. It is the *man* that perceives, and loves and hates, and acts; not his understanding, or his heart, or his will, distinct from himself.[34]

Asa Burton, of Vermont, is generally regarded as the "Father" of the school. He described a faculty as "a preparedness in the mind for certain operations."[35]

What was really distinctive about this school was their insistence that the human will is the capacity of the mind to act, to perform the functions to which it is directed by the sensibility. Albert T. Bledsoe, a Philadelphia lawyer and mathematics teacher, contrasted the roles of the two powers.

The truth is, that in feeling the mind is passive; and it is absurd to make a passive impression the active cause of any thing. The sensibility does not *act*, it merely *suffers*. The appetites and passions, which have always been called the 'active powers,' the 'moving principles,' and so forth, should be called the passive susceptibilities . . . the will [is] the *active power*.[36]

As Burton saw it, the will is simply an "executive faculty" under the control of the heart. He leaves little doubt as to the character of the actions carried out by the will: "The immediate object of volition is generally the motion of the whole body, or some one of its members."[37]

This is one of the clearest cases of the usage of will as a dynamic power. The active faculty is precisely the power to move one's body at the behest of one's feelings. It is in this sense that the Faculty Psychologists use the term "will" in arguing against Jonathan Edwards' alleged determinism. In effect, these faculty theorists say: everyone knows that he is in control of the movements of his own body; this is the proof that man's will is free.

Somewhat the same meaning is given to will in the writings

of Alexander Bain. This British thinker is one of the last figures in the Associationist school. He differentiates feelings from volitions. Primary and simple feelings are called sensations; secondary and compound feelings are emotions. Will, as Bain sees it, comprises two aspects: a certain spontaneity of movement and some sort of linking of movement with feelings of pleasure and pain.[38] Only some actions of the human body are will-actions: these stem from feelings. Bain sometimes offers an explanation of willing which is rather physiological.

Will or volition comprises all the actions of human beings in so far as impelled or guided by Feelings. Eating, walking, building, sowing, speaking—are actions performed with some *end* in view; and ends are comprised in the gaining of pleasure or the avoiding of pain. Actions not prompted by feelings are not voluntary. Such are the powers of nature—wind, gravity, electricity, etc.; so also the organic functions of breathing, circulation, and the movements of the intestines.[39]

Will is not a power, in any sense, for Bain. It is involved with the explanation of man's activities (and that is why his view is treated in this chapter), but Bain's will is some sort of connection or association that develops after spontaneous movements of the body have been performed for some time. An awareness develops that certain actions promote feelings of pleasure; when such activities are continued or repeated, they are said to be willed.[40] There is not much difference between Bain's meaning of will and Pavlov's conditioned reflexes, except for the fact that the Russian dealt with dogs.

There is little tendency in French usage to identify will with a dynamic power causing movements in the human body. Maine de Biran had insisted that will is a spiritual energy. He criticized a contemporary attempt to relate willing to bodily functions.

The vain effort tried by one of the most distinguished physiologists of our day to force the inclusion of the immediate products of the will in the symmetrical framework of vital functions or properties brings out with new clarity the hyper-organic and super-animal character of this intelligent force whose acts or special attributes are so clearly distinguished from all that can be referred to the organism or animality.[41]

However, it is as "force" that Maine de Biran thinks of will. Will or volition (*vouloir*) is the free activity of the personal self.

This notion of will as a capacity for mental activity, different from abstract intelligence, continues in nineteenth-century French thought. It is combined with the notion of will as a "power"—a borrowing by men like Royer-Collard, Théodore Jouffroy and Victor Cousin from the Scotch "common-sense" school.[42] Thus, even today, a standard French dictionary of philosophical terms identifies will and the faculty of activity.[43] One way in which Henri Bergson described "intuition" was as, "that faculty of seeing which is immanent in the faculty of acting and which springs, in some way, from the turning of the function of willing (*de la torsion du vouloir*) upon itself."[44] Bergson's notion of vital force (*élan vital*) is closely related to his meaning of will. It is, as R. B. Perry has pointed out, in the "higher flights" of the *élan vital*, "in thought, morality, art, and religion," that Bergson recognizes it as will.[45] Maurice Blondel is another example of a philosopher who identifies will with the capacity for action; his whole philosophy was built on this idea.[46]

Twentieth-century usage in the United States often con-

nects willing with the putting forth of *effort*. This meaning
is much stressed by William James. He came under the strong
influence of Charles Renouvier and the activist notion of will
that we have seen in the French philosophy of the spirit.[47]
However, James was interested in relating willing to bodily
activity in a way that was foreign to French spiritualism. This
physiological bent is illustrated in the following passage:

Our sensations and thoughts are but cross-sections, as it were,
of currents whose essential consequence is motion, and which no
sooner run in at one nerve than they run out at another. The
popular notion that mere consciousness as such is not a forerunner
of activity, that the latter must result from some superadded 'will-
force,' is a very natural inference from those special cases in
which we think of an act for an indefinite length of time without
the action taking place. These cases, however, are not the norm;
they are cases of inhibition by antagonistic thoughts. When the
blocking is released we feel as if an inward spring were let loose,
and this is the additional impulse of *fiat* upon which the act effec-
tively succeeds.[48]

As this explanation indicates, James did not give a simple
"dynamic-power" meaning to will. He thought that willing is
a mental function, a relation between the mind and its ideas.
The effect of volition is "the prevalence of the idea."[49] That a
certain idea endures and stands out in conscious experience is
due to interest, attention and consent. When James had indicated these factors of willing, he was still left with the feeling
that there is something more to it, something which he could
only call effort. So, James can say: "Effort is thus the essential
phenomenon of will."[50]

This same emphasis on effort is found in recent Soviet psychologies of will. This is the first point that is made by Jozef
Reutt, in his summary of Russian thinking on the question.

Soviet psychology recognizes the existence of will as an indispensable part of psychic life and stresses most decidedly its significance for the evolution of man, for the development of his character and mind. It also links the will of man with his activities as an absolutely necessary and ever present factor in human life.

According to Soviet psychologists a characteristic feature of volitional actions is the fact that they are connectd with the overcoming of obstacles. In consequence of this fact appears effort which represents the most essential feature of all processes of will.[51]

Much stress is placed on "will power" and its increase, by endeavoring to control the self, by much hard work, and by participation in community efforts.[52] The training of the will of the child is an important aspect of Soviet educational psychology.[53]

This very practical and simple meaning of will is not far removed from the usage of American pragmatism and naturalism. To will is to make a personal effort. John Dewey is in this activist tradition, when he says that will is:

the body of habits, of active dispositions which makes a man do what he does. Will is thus not something opposed to consequences; it is causation in its personal aspect, the aspect immediately preceding action. It hardly seems conceivable to practical sense that by will is meant something which can be complete without reference to deeds prompted and results occasioned.[54]

Some of this dynamic meaning of volition is a carry-over from Dewey's early period, in which he was much influenced by German idealism. In 1887, his *Psychology* showed this commitment.

We find the unity of the psychical processes . . . and therefore their ultimate explanation, in the fact that man is a self; that the essence of self is the self-determining activity of will; that this will is an objectifying activity, and that, in objectifying itself, it renders itself universal. The result of this activity is knowledge.[55]

Josiah Royce could have written these same words; the identification of will with personal energy was common in much American philosophy at the beginning of this century.

Twentieth-century Italian thought also understands will (*volontà*) in terms of personal activity. Under the influence of Fichte, Schelling and Hegel, and consciously going back to the theory of art of Giambattista Vico, Italian neo-idealism asserted that all reality is of the nature of "spirit" and all activity is volitional.[56] In spite of personal differences, Benedetto Croce and Giovanni Gentile shared this point of view. As far as Croce is concerned, spiritual activity is always an act of volition, either utilitarian (economic) or moral (ethical).[57] The only exception would be in the sphere of artistic creativity, where cognitive action is dominant. In the case of Gentile, spirit is more personal; I actively create my own world. Nevertheless, the action of my spirit is will.

Spirit is the only reality and its reality is its activity, the activity by which he knows is the very activity by which he is ever creating the world, that is, his own very self; and thus every knowing is a willing and every willing is a knowing, and Spirit appears as a knowing-doing creative activity.[58]

Much the same meaning is given to will in the writings of Ugo Spirito.[59]

Contemporary work in experimental psychology has little to say about the meaning of will. Usually the language of willing is avoided by psychologists. There are studies of motivation, decision-making, problem-solving, choosing, and so on, but this experimental work is not related to what the philosopher and the ordinary man still call will.[60] Mention has been made earlier of certain experimental studies of volitional activity which were conducted in Germany, Belgium and England, during the first three decades of this century. This work used the introspective methods of Narziss Ach and A. E. Michotte.[61] Several books were published in English by psychologists who worked under these men or carried on similar experiments.[62] In general, this movement identified will with the capacity to make choices but it also placed some emphasis on will as an active power which enables man to overcome obstacles and to put forth personal effort. One gets the impression that these people approached the experimental study of volition with a preconceived philosophical notion of what will is and then found that their laboratory investigations did little to confirm or negate this assumed meaning. A typical summary statement is found in a book by Boyd Barrett:

Many words and phrases denote volitional activities. 'To make up one's mind,' to resolve, to consent, to desire, to strive, to choose, to make an effort—these infinitives point to will acts. Conation, intention, willing, inhibiting, controlling, permitting, preventing, and many such words are also used of the will. When a man of character, at some crisis of his life, *makes up his mind* to adopt a certain course, and says, 'I will do so and so. I am determined to do it. It is my firm intention to do it'—he is speaking of a certain state of soul that we call *willing*. This state is radically different from all other states. It is about action. It concerns self and is very personal. It is a law and a line of conduct. It binds and controls. It is creative and arbitrary. It means self determination. Self rules self. It is about the future. It is about reality. It is something almost sacred.[63]

That Boyd Barrett thought of will as a dynamic power is rather evident from the foregoing; in fact, his book is entitled, *Strength of Will*.

An American psychologist, Raymond H. Wheeler, conducted similar experimental studies in this country, in 1920, and concluded that there is no definite experience of willing or choosing, as such. He claimed that his subjects were aware only of physical and sensory processes.[64] Mary W. Calkins criticized his interpretation and insisted that Wheeler's subjects, and her own subjects in similar experiments, did experience a kind of self-activity that could be called volition.[65] It may be noted that Miss Calkins had a definite philosophical commitment to Personalism.[66]

The literature of clinical psychology and some branches of psychiatry offers occasional studies of will and its relation to emotional disorders and mental abnormalities.[67] Will appears to be understood as the capacity to make a personal effort or to establish some goal in life. Of course, Otto Rank calls his method of treatment "Will Therapy"—in reaction to both Freudian and Adlerian psychiatric techniques—and has written extensively on this subject.[68] In spite of its central position in his therapy, it is difficult to determine just what will means to Rank. He makes it very clear, however, that Freud neglected the human will (whatever it is) and that Alfred Adler overstressed the "Will to Power."[69] In fact, it is not unfair to conclude that, if you wish to find out what will means, do not ask psychologists or psychiatrists.

The meaning that we have seen throughout this chapter identifies will with the soul or mind of man as acting. Sometimes the results of such volitional activity are purely immaterial; sometimes they are physical. Will is thus understood as energy, activity itself, personal dynamism or power. This way of using the language of volition usually emphasizes freedom as a concomitant of such activity—but this is not true in all authors. Hobbes is a notable exception. The notion of will as the executive power, under the control of the heart, is a very special case of the dynamic power theory.

NOTES

1. Plotinus, *Enneads,* IV, 3, 23 (ed. Bréhier, IV, 90).

2. In *Ennead* IV, 3, 25 (ed. Bréhier, IV, 94, line 9), sensation is attributed to a *koinon ergon,* a common energy, of soul and body.

3. Cf. G. Verbeke, *L'Evolution de la doctrine du Pneuma,* p. 78.

4. Matt. 6:10. In the Greek version (*genetheto to thelema sou*) "will" is not *boulesis* but *thelema,* and the verb may not be quite so suggestive of activity. See: *St. Luke's Gospel* (Greek Text), ed. J. T. White (London: Longmans, Green, 1909), p. 55.

5. St. Augustine, *De civitate Dei,* XIV, 6.

6. St. Augustine, *De diversis quaestionibus,* q. VIII (ed. Maur. Venetiis, 1731, VI, 3 C–D).

7. *De quantitate animae,* 21, 35 (ed. Maur., I, 418).

8. Richard Fishacre's *Commentary on the Sentences, MS Paris. Nat. lat.,* 15754, fol. 181va–181vb, is unedited; my citation is from a portion of his text, printed in Lottin, *Psychologie et Morale,* III (2), p. 408: "cum sint tantum duo principia agentia tamquam due cause efficientes, scilicet natura et voluntas; hec utraque conjuncta reperiuntur in anima . . . licet utrumque sit agens, et natura et voluntas, tamen potentior est voluntas et magis activa quam natura in nobis."

9. Bradwardine, *De causa Dei adversus Pelagium,* I, 10 (the text from p. 195 B, of the printing of London, 1618, is quoted in Ueberweg-Geyer, *Geschichte der Philosophie,* zweiter Teil, Berlin: Mittler, 1928, p. 623): "Divina voluntas est causa efficiens cujuslibet rei factae, movens seu motrix cujuslibet motionis."

10. *De causa Dei,* III, 1 (p. 637 D, in the ed. of London, 1618, cited in Ueberweg-Geyer, p. 623).

11. F. Bacon, *De dignitate et augmentis scientiarum* (written A.D. 1623), II, 13; see the analysis in Alexander, *Theories of Will,* p. 160.

12. Hobbes, *Concerning Body,* II, 10, 7; in *English Works,* ed. Molesworth (London: Bohn and Longmans, 1839–1845), vol. I, 132.

13. Hobbes, *Leviathan*, I, 6; *English Works*, ed. Molesworth, III, 47–49.

14. *Concerning Body, IV*, 25, 13; *English Works*, I, 409.

15. *Ibid.*, IV, 25, 2; *English Works*, I, 389.

16. G. Berkeley, *Alciphron*, VII, 18–20; *Works*, ed. A. A. Luce and T. E. Jessop, London: Nelson, 1948–1957, vol. III.

17. Berkeley, *Principles of Human Knowledge*, 27; *Works*, vol. II.

18. On this problem in the phenomenalism of Hume, see: J. Collins, *A History of Modern European Philosophy*, pp. 406–410.

19. J. Locke, *Essay concerning Human Understanding*, II, 21, 31: "This uneasiness we may call, as it is, *desire;* which is an uneasiness of the mind for want of some absent good."

20. D. Hume, *Treatise of Human Nature*, II, 3, 1; ed. Selby-Bigge (Oxford: Clarendon Press, 1888), p. 399.

21. *Ibid.*, II, 3, 2; Selby-Bigge, p. 407; where Hume also speaks of liberty of indifference as a "negation of necessity and causes." Cf. *Enquiry concerning the Human Understanding*, VIII, 2, second ed. by Selby-Bigge (Oxford: Clarendon Press, 1902), p. 95.

22. Appendix I, *Concerning Moral Sentiment*, in *An Enquiry concerning the Principles of Morals* (written 1751), explains these associations in the moral situation; see *Hume Selections*, ed. C. W. Hendel (New York: Scribner, 1927), pp. 238–245.

23. J. S. Mill, *A System of Logic* (New York: Harper and Bros., 1884), p. 256; cf. *Examination of Sir William Hamilton's Philosophy*, 2 vols. (New York: Holt, 1874), II, 279.

24. T. Reid, *Essays on the Active Powers of Man*, in *Works*, ed. W. Hamilton (Edinburgh: Maclachlan, Stewart and Co., 1846), pp. 530–531.

25. I. Kant, *Fundamental Principles of the Metaphysic of Morals*, trans. Abbott, p. 63.

26. F. W. Schelling, *System des transcendentalen Idealismus* (Tübingen, 1800), trans. in *Journal of Speculative Philosophy*, I (1867), 159–165; the quotation is from Robinson, *Anthology of Modern Philosophy* (New York: Crowell, 1931), p. 569.

27. J. G. Fichte, *Vocation of Man*, in the trans. by William Smith (London: Trübner, 1889); quotation from Robinson, *op. cit.*, p. 557.

28. A. Schopenhauer, *The World as Will and Idea*, trans. Haldane and Kemp (London: Kegan Paul, 1907–1909), vol. I, 143.

29. F. Nietzsche, *Jenseits von Gut und Böse*, ch. 36; the translation is from *Works*, ed. O. Levy, trans. H. Zimmern (Edinburgh-London: T. N. Foulis, 1911), vol. XII, 52.

30. R. H. Lotze, *Microcosmos*, trans. E. Hamilton and E. E. C.

Jones (New York: Scribner, 1887), I, 148. On Lotze's psychology, see: G. Stanley-Hall, *Founders of Modern Psychology* (New York: D. Appleton, 1912), pp. 65–121.

31. *Microcosmos*, trans. Hamilton-Jones, I, 286.

32. *Ibid.*

33. On the Faculty Psychologists, see: J. Wharton Fay, *American Psychology before William James* (New Brunswick: Rutgers U. Press, 1939) (with an excellent bibliography); H. W. Schneider, *A History of American Philosophy* (New York: Columbia University Press, 1946), pp. 232–237. For two contrasting accounts of will in this school: F. H. Foster, *A Genetic History of the New England Theology* (Chicago: University of Chicago Press, 1907), ch. IX: The Development of the Theory of the Will; and J. Haroutunian, *Piety Versus Moralism* (New York: Holt, 1932), ch. IX: The Freedom of the Power of the Faculty of Will.

34. J. Day, *An Enquiry Respecting the Self-Determining Power of the Will* (New Haven: Yale University Press, 1838), p. 40.

35. A. Burton, *Essays on Some of the First Principles of Metaphysicks, Ethicks, and Theology* (Portland: Arthur Shirley, 1824). These essays were written twenty years earlier.

36. A. T. Bledsoe, *An Examination of President Edwards' Inquiry into the Freedom of the Will* (Philadelphia, 1845), pp. 101–102.

37. Burton, *op. cit.*, p. 85. On the next page he says: "The body and its members are, in general, under the control of the will."

38. A. Bain, *The Emotions and the Will* (New York: D. Appleton, 1888), p. 303.

39. Bain, *Mental and Moral Science* (London: Longmans, 1868), p. 2.

40. *The Emotions and the Will*, p. 321.

41. Maine de Biran, *Nouveaux essais d'anthropologie*, in *Oeuvres*, ed. Tisserand, XIV, 311.

42. Cf. J. Peghaire, "Peut-on encore parler des facultés de l'âme?" *Revue de l'Université d'Ottawa* (1941), p. 124.

43. A. Lalande, *Vocabulaire technique et critique de la philosophie*, 4me éd. (Paris: Société Française de Philosophie, 1938), vol. I, 237.

44. H. Bergson, *Evolution créatrice* (Paris: Alcan, 1907), p. 272.

45. R. B. Perry, *Philosophy of the Recent Past* (New York: Scribner, 1926), p. 174.

46. Cf. J. Havet, "French Philosophical Tradition between the Two Wars," in *Philosophic Thought in France and the United States* (Buffalo: University of Buffalo Press, 1950), pp. 8–9.

47. R. B. Perry, *The Thought and Character of William James*,

2 vols. (Boston: Little, Brown, 1936), I, 655: "That Renouvier was the greatest individual influence upon the development of James' thought cannot be doubted."

48. W. James, *Principles of Psychology*, 2 vols. (New York: Holt, 1890), II, 526–527.

49. *Ibid.*, p. 560.

50. *Ibid.*, II, 562. An earlier article by James, "What the Will Effects," *Scribner's Magazine*, III (1888), 240–250, had stressed the notion of effort.

51. J. Reutt, "Psychologia woli w nauce radzieckiej," *Przeglad Psychologiszny*, I (1952), 58–113; the quotation is from the English Summary, p. 226.

52. *Ibid.*, pp. 229–232.

53. K. I. Lebeden, "K Voprosu ob Izlozhenii Teorii Voli v Uchebnikakh Psikhlogii," *Sovietskaya Pedagogia*, I (1950), 64–67; on the problem of presenting a theory of will in psychology textbooks.

54. J. Dewey, *Human Nature and Conduct* (New York: Holt, 1922), p. 44.

55. Dewey, *Psychology* (New York: Harper, 1887), p. 423.

56. Cf. A. Crespi, *Contemporary Thought of Italy* (New York: Knopf, 1926), pp. 40–66; E. Chiocchetti, *La Filosofia di Benedetto Croce* (Milano: Vita e Pensiero, 1924), pp. 51–74.

57. "Nessun fatto dello spirito, ossia nessuna manifestazione di attività si puo addure, che, esaminata non superficialmente, non si riduca a un atto di fantasia, di intelletto e di percezione (che è, precisamente, visione dell'individuale nei suoi rapporti universali); ovvero a un atto di volizione utilitaria o etica." B. Croce, *Filosofia della pratica*, II, 1 (Bari: Laterza, 1923), p. 225.

58. This passage is evidently from G. Gentile, *Il pensiero come atto puro* (Messina, 1923); it is quoted without any reference, in Crespi, *op. cit.*, p. 152.

59. U. Spirito, "L'Uomo e la Natura," *Atti del XII Congresso di Filosofia* (Firenze: Sansoni, 1960), II, 411–418.

60. For some examples of early twentieth-century psychological views, see C. E. Skinner, *Readings in Psychology* (New York: Farrar and Rinehart, 1935), "Volition," pp. 647–678. There is practically nothing on the subject in E. G. Boring, *A History of Experimental Psychology* (New York: Appleton-Century-Crofts, 1950).

61. N. Ach, *Ueber die Willenstätigkeit und das Denken* (Göttingen: Vandenhoech und Ruprecht, 1905); A. Michotte et E. Prüm, "Etude expérimentale sur le choix voluntaire," *Archives de Psychologie*, X (1910–1911), 113–320.

62. Examples of such publications are: E. Boyd Barrett, *Motive-force and Motivation-tracks* (London: Longmans, Green, 1911); R. McCarthy, *The Measurement of Conation* (Chicago: Loyola University Press, 1926); J. Lindworsky, *The Training of the Will*, trans. A. Steiner and E. A. Fitzpatrick (Milwaukee: Bruce, 1929); F. Aveling, *Personality and Will* (New York; D. Appleton, 1931).

63. E. Boyd Barrett, *Strength of Will* (New York: Kenedy, 1915), p. 41.

64. R. H. Wheeler, *Experimental Investigation of the Process of Choosing* (Eugene, Oregon: University of Oregon Publication, 1920); cf. Wheeler, "Analyzed and Unanalyzed Experience," *Psychological Review*, 29 (1922), 425–446.

65. M. W. Calkins, "Fact and Inference in R. Wheeler's Doctrine of Will and Self-Activity," *Psychological Review*, 28 (1921), 356–374.

66. See: Calkins, "The Philosophic 'credo' of an Absolutistic Personalist," in *Contemporary American Philosophy*, ed. Adams and Montague (New York: Macmillan, 1930), I, 197–217.

67. Cf. A. Wheelis, "Will and Psychoanalysis," *Journal of the American Psychoanalytic Association*, IV (1956), 285–303; E. M. Scott, "Will and Religion as Useful Adjuncts in Psychotherapy," *Psychical Reports*, I (1955), 379–381; E. Forti, "Les déreglements de la volonté et leur interprétation psychologique," *Egyptian Journal of Psychology*, VIII (1952), 117–138; P. Mullahy, "Will, Choice, and Ends," *Psychiatry*, XII (1949), 379–386.

68. O. Rank, *Modern Education: A Critique* (New York: Knopf, 1932), ch. III: Training of the Will and Emotional Development; *Will Therapy and Truth and Reality* (New York: Knopf, 1950).

69. Cf. A. Adler, *The Practise and Theory of Individual Psychology* (New York: Harcourt, Brace, 1924), 2nd ed., 1927. A quick sketch of the Will to Power, as "a primitive tendency of human nature," is found in R. Allers, *Psychology of Character* (New York: Sheed & Ward, 1939), pp. 28–30.

CHAPTER VI

Heart, Affection and Will

IN THIS CHAPTER, we shall examine a theory of will in which love is taken as the central or distinctive function of volition. Such a view is often associated with the use of the term, heart, either as the equivalent of will or the organ of volition, or as distinguished from will in some significant way. In the latter sense, we shall see that some thinkers regard the human will as the executive of the heart's feelings.

There appear to be two ancient sources of this use of the "heart-language" in association with willing and loving. These are the Bible and ancient Greek medicine. In the *Septuagint*, we find numerous texts such as the following:

And God seeing that the wickedness of men was great on earth, and that all the thought of their heart was bent upon evil at all times, it repented him that he had made man on the earth. (Genesis 6:5–6)

. . . for the imagination and thought of man's heart are prone to evil from his youth. (Genesis 8:21)

Open not thy heart to every man: lest he repay thee with an evil turn, and speak reproachfully to thee. (Ecclesiasticus 8:22)

In ancient Hebrew usage, the word *heart* (*leb*) means the center in man's personality from which freely spring thoughts, decisions and aspirations. As Tresmontant explains it:

'Heart' in the Bible does not, as in our Western tradition, mean the affections, sensibility as opposed to reason. It is rather man's liberty, the centre in which are taken the fundamental decisions. . . . Thoughts arise in the heart (*alah al leb*) out of an original freedom that engenders them.[1]

Because of this, the Greek *Septuagint* often uses the word, *nous* (intelligence), where the Hebrew would have heart (*leb*).[2] Indeed, the biblical use of heart seems to cover all the higher functions of the human soul.

We find much the same heart-language in the New Testament. There is a passage in St. Paul where nearly all the traditional functions of the "heart" are mentioned. He commences by saying: "Brethren, the will of my heart, indeed, and my prayer to God is for them unto salvation." And later in the same chapter, he adds: "For if thou confess with thy mouth the Lord Jesus and believe in thy heart that God hath raised him up from the dead, thou shalt be saved. For, with the heart, we believe unto justice."[3] Here we have both will and belief associated with heart. There is no question, then, that the Bible has influenced our use of the term, heart, in this way.

One important school of Greek medicine was that which flourished in Sicily during the third century before Christ. According to Werner Jaeger, a leading doctor in this school was Diokles of Karystos who was contemporary with the establishment of the Stoic school of philosophy and may have influenced it.[4] Now, Diokles taught that man's heart is the organic center of human personality, the principle of motor activity and perception in man. This teaching is connected with the Stoic view that there is a ruling principle (the *hegemonikon* or *pneuma psychikon*) within the human person.[5] As a matter of fact, Aristotle also situated the "spirit" in the human heart and his view may have influenced these thinkers in the century following him.[6] This theory was quite different from that of the Hippocratic medical school, in which the brain was taken as the central organ of the vital spirit. It is not clear whether the Sicilian doctors or the Athenian philosophers first emphasized the importance of the heart, for there was a fourth-century physician, named Philistion, who visited Athens during the period of Plato and the young Aristotle and who may have given the theory to them.[7] In any case, the medical view that the heart is the key organ of man's higher thought and will processes continued to be influential during the middle ages, through various Arabic and Latin treatises, *On the Motion of the Heart*. The heart was not regarded as a blood pump, of course, but as the center from which emanated various humors, or animal spirits, which affected human personality.

Most serious writers in the Patristic and medieval periods use the word, heart, to name that part of man in which he loves, believes, decides, regrets and rejoices. The same thinkers recognize that these are, in the main, volitional functions. The notion of "heart" becomes dissociated from the concept of a bodily organ and is spiritualized, or transferred to the psychic order, but there always remains in the background some vestige of the theory that these operations of will are located in the breast, or in the region of the organic heart. The continued use in pictorial art of the heart symbol is but one evidence of this conviction. There would be no advantage in attempting to name or quote all the writers who employ this heart-language. We have no difficulty in finding a few outstanding examples.

What is the best remembered quotation from all the writings of St. Augustine? Doubtless it is his poignant cry, at the beginning of the *Confessions*: "restless is my heart until it

finds rest in Thee." The full Latin text shows how Augustine
here connects the heart with functions of willing and loving.
What he actually wrote was:

Et tamen laudare te vult homo, aliqua portio creaturae tuae. Tu
excitas ut laudare te delectet, quia fecisti nos ad te et inquietum
est cor nostrum, donec requiescat in te.[8]

Augustine is praising God and he says that man is stimulated
by God, so that a person wills to love God and takes a real
joy in praising his Maker. Man has been created with a strong
inclination toward God and this heartfelt urge is unsatisfied,
until man achieves some sort of loving union with God.
Clearly, the human heart is regarded by Augustine as the
seat of man's highest aspirations and his most spiritual loves.
In a later work, the great treatise *On the Trinity*, Augustine
explained that he understood love (*amor seu dilectio*) to be
but a strong form of willing (*valentior voluntas*).[9] There is
no doubt that St. Augustine closely related the will of man to
his heart.

There is a tenth-century Jewish treatise, entitled *The Book
of Beliefs and Opinions*.[10] Its writer, Saadia ben Joseph, was
born in A.D. 892, at Fajjum, Egypt. He says that the human
soul, in union with the body, has three faculties: the power
of knowing (*nešamah*), the power of appetition (*nepheš*), and
the power of anger (*ruaḥ*).[11] This psychological analysis is
thoroughly developed by Saadia. Then he points out that
Scripture invariably mentions soul and heart together and
adds that the seal of the human soul is in the heart.[12]

A twelfth-century Spanish Jew, Bahya ibn Pakuda, wrote
a moral treatise entitled, *Duties of the Heart* (*Hovot Haleva-
vot*), in which the heart is formally taken as the center of

man's love for God. One sentence is perhaps enough to indicate the tenor of the work:

When the believer's heart has been emptied of love of this world and freed from its lusts, as a result of perception and understanding [the love of God is] established in his heart and fixed in his soul.[13]

Some Christian theologians in the twelfth century show a tendency to distinguish two "wills" in man: the affective will (*voluntas affectionis*) which gives rise to man's interior feelings of love and other volitional functions; and the effective will (*voluntas effectionis*) which is directed to exterior, volitionally controlled human actions.[14] The inner volitional feelings are said to be meritorious (in relation to eventual salvation), while the volitional control of bodily actions is called a perfectant of merit.[15] This distinction is not, to my knowledge, associated with references to the heart but it does indicate a growing interest in those aspects of willing that have to do with love and affection.

One key characteristic of Franciscan psychology in the thirteenth and fourteenth centuries is a certain quality that is called "unction." It means that men like John of La Rochelle, St. Bonaventure, Matthew of Aquasparta, Duns Scotus and even William of Ockham put particular stress on the love of God and on the affective dispositions of man. The views of St. Bonaventure may be taken as typical of this school in the thirteenth century. He is contemporary with Thomas Aquinas and read much the same literature that Aquinas knew. However, Bonaventure's psychology is not the same as that which Aquinas developed. The Franciscans are usually closer to the thought of St. Augustine.

For one thing, Bonaventure speaks of intellect and will as

different potencies of the human soul but he does not radically
distinguish volition from intellection. As Robert Kilwardby
(a Dominican scholar who agreed with many philosophical
views of the Franciscan school) was to say in the 1270's, to
know and to love are one and the same act of the soul.[16] St.
Bonaventure shows this attitude in the way that he treats
synderesis. Thomas Aquinas considered synderesis to be a
habit in the practical intellect whereby man knows, from the
beginning of his life of moral reasoning, such practical principles as the rule that "good should be done and evil avoided."
Now Bonaventure located synderesis in the will and treated
this habit of first practical principles as an affective tendency
toward the good and away from the evil. He called synderesis
a "weight of the will," inclining man toward the moral good.[17]
This tendency to fuse volition, affection and cognition was
continued and emphasized by a group of British thinkers at
Oxford, in the early fourteenth century. Their writings are
only available in manuscript form but they have been very
thoroughly studied by the Polish medievalist, Konstantin
Michalski.[18] A certain Adam Woodham was the central figure
in this movement to attribute a wide variety of cognitive activities, judgment, evaluation, a sort of discursive reasoning,
to the human will. Their contemporaries at Paris (men like
Gregory of Rimini, John of Ripa and Pierre d'Ailly) strongly
opposed this tendency. But eventually some continental
thinkers, who are not Franciscans, come to tolerate and even
to espouse the notion that the will is able to know things. John
of Mirecourt (*monachus albus*) is skeptical of the view but
decides that neither side of the argument can be proved.
Hugolinus de Malabranca, O.S.A., favors the Oxford theory
and teaches that there are two kinds of knowledge through
the will: (1) an "experimental" knowledge of the immediately

present object of volition; and (2) an "affective" knowledge of a remembered act of willing.[19]

On another point St. Bonaventure has a very distinctive position on the human will: he thinks that there are two appetites within the will, one is concupiscible and the other is irascible.[20] These are not separate, sensory appetites but divisions of will itself. As a consequence, Bonaventure is able to attribute a wide variety of feelings or affections to the human will.

If we look at the fifteenth-century *Book on the Soul*, in which William of Vaurouillon summarized many of the earlier Franciscan psychological positions, we see these views as characteristic of a continuing school. Moreover, William discusses the problem of the assigning of an organic base for the sensory feelings of desire and anger. He reports that some people have located the concupiscible appetite in the liver (*jecur*) and the irascible in the gall bladder (*cista fellis*), but William gives it as his opinion that both are more truly located in the heart.[21]

As far as the use of the term, heart, is concerned, this continues to be a common feature, particularly in works of piety. Even Thomas Aquinas (who is not much given to romantic metaphors) will occasionally refer volitional activities to the heart. A test case may be made of his treatment of charity, the love of God for His own sake and the love of creatures for the sake of God. In the *Questions on the Virtues in General*, Aquinas carefully explains that there are two major virtues that have the will of man as their subject; these are justice and charity.[22] Earlier, in commenting on the third book of the *Sentences*, he had calmly said, with St. Paul: "Hence, we must say that charity is a theological virtue that is, 'poured forth into our hearts by the Holy Spirit who has been given to us.' "[23]

Modern philosophy is equally broad-minded in attributing love, affection and other volitional functions to the human heart. In a famous passage, Shakespeare sets the pattern in English writings by locating passion in the blood:

> Paris and Troilus, you have both said well;
> And on the cause and question now in hand
> Have gloz'd, but superficially; not much
> Unlike young men, whom Aristotle thought
> Unfit to hear moral philosophy.
> The reasons you allege do more conduce
> To the hot passion of distemper'd blood
> Than to make up a free determination
> 'Twixt right and wrong; for pleasure and revenge
> Have ears more deaf than adders to the voice
> Of any true decision.[24]

Shakespeare's philosophical contemporary, Thomas Hobbes, does not write as well but is equally sure that the heart is the seat of the affections. Hobbes explains the whole thing very simply:

Conceptions or apparitions are nothing really, but motion in some internal substance of the head; which motion not stopping there, but proceeding to the heart, of necessity must there either help or hinder that motion which is called vital; when it helpeth, it is called DELIGHT, contentment, or pleasure, which is nothing really but motion about the heart, as conception is nothing but motion within the head; . . . but when such motion weakeneth or hindereth the vital motion, then it is called PAIN. . . . This motion, in which consisteth pleasure or pain, is also a solicitation or provocation either to draw near to the thing that pleaseth, or to retire from the thing that displeaseth. And this solicitation is the endeavour or internal beginning of animal motion, which when the object delighteth, is called APPETITE; when it displeaseth, it is called AVERSION.[25]

Perhaps no other serious writer has so baldly reduced man's emotional and volitional life to a mere fluttering of the heart, which in Hobbes' view is certainly the physical organ in the human breast.

John Locke has nothing to do with the crude corporealism of Hobbes but he does root man's volitional activity in the affective functions. He thinks that the psychic motivation for willing to act is always a certain feeling which he calls "uneasiness."[26] These psychic functions occur in what Locke vaguely terms, the mind. Bishop Berkeley calls it "spirit" and insists on its unity and simplicity. Though he occasionally mentions the heart, Berkeley does not think of it as a special power of affection or decision. As he sees it, "A spirit is one simple, undivided, active being: as it perceives ideas, it is called the *understanding*, and as it produces or otherwise operates about them, it is called *will*."[27] David Hume puts the source of volitional activity in a felt impression that one has of giving rise to a new motion in the body or the mind.[28] However, Hume continually speaks of the heart as the seat of human feelings[29] and he has one lyric sentence in which he seems to say that the heart intuits moral values: "What is honourable, what is fair, what is becoming, what is noble, what is generous, takes possession of the heart, and animates us to embrace and maintain it."[30]

What we have seen in this quick survey of British philosophy is a gradual but persistent tendency to place some sort of feeling before the movements of the human will. Whether or not these feelings or affections are located in the heart is not of primary importance. The important thing is that willing becomes an activity motivated by a prior feeling. With the

development of Associationism, there is no longer any suggestion that feelings actually *cause* volitions. Instead, will
comes to be regarded as a spontaneous capacity or tendency to
personal movement, sometimes following feeling, sometimes
not. As Alexander Bain describes it, the affective control of
will is simply the result of repetition of situations in which
willing follows feeling. He says:

I shall examine at length the two fundamental component elements of the Will. . . . These are, first, the existence of a spontaneous tendency to execute movements independent of the stimulus
of sensations or feelings; and secondly, the link between a present
action and a present feeling, whereby the one comes under the
control of the other.[31]

In this psychology, will in its strongest sense is the executive
function of carrying out in action the demands of human
feelings. Volition is made a mere application of the Associationist law of self-conservation. Here again, Bain gives the
accepted explanation:

The link between feeling and action is traced to the law that
connects pleasure with increased vitality—the law of Self-
Conservation. From this root there are two branches, which
diverge, but yet occasionally come together. One branch is the
proper emotional manifestations, the other enters into volition.[32]

Continental European philosophy, from Descartes to Hegel,
offers no parallel examples of the foregoing British trend
toward a position in which feeling becomes a guide for will-
activity. The French and German thinkers have their own
theories on the nature of human feelings or emotions. These
they usually develop in treatises or portions of works, entitled, "On the Passions of the Soul." Perhaps the Continentals

are more traditional than their British contemporaries, in thinking that man's emotional life requires to be controlled by reason or will, rather than the opposite. Perhaps the Greek respect for the rule of reason is more persistent on the Continent than in England. In any case, early modern philosophy in Europe places little stress on the role of love and affection in the practical life of man. The term, heart, is used in the psychic sense, of course. Rousseau relates it to moral conscience and clearly distinguishes it from mere feeling, in the following passage from his novel, *Emile*:

Conscience is the voice of the soul, the passions are the voice of the body. . . . Conscience never deceives us; she is the true guide of man; it is to the soul what instinct is to the body; he who obeys his conscience is following nature. . . . There is therefore at the bottom of our hearts an innate principle of justice and virtue, by which, in spite of our maxims, we judge our own actions or those of others to be good or evil; and it is this principle that I call conscience.[33]

In German philosophy after Hegel, there is a strong reaction against his abstractness and rationalistic system-building. A romantic German school develops which takes love as the key activity of the human will and soul. Friedrich von Schlegel represents this movement, at the beginning of the nineteenth century. He says that the "soul is nothing less than the faculty of love in man."[34] Four faculties are distinguished in man: understanding, will, reason and fancy. Conflicts occur among these powers and Schlegel attributes this friction to the results of the Fall of man. On this score, he compares man unfavorably with the angels:

With them [the angels] understanding and willing are altogether one. . . . Their activity is ever one and the same living and uninter-

rupted operation. . . . And thus it is that with these spirits knowing and willing are one; so that a living and effective intellect is
even a very spirit, and equally so is a perfectly self-conscious
will. But a spiritual being like man, in whom intellect and will are
not one, is, as contemplated from this point of view, a spirit
divided and distracted.[35]

Schlegel's prescription for the unification and harmoniza-
tion of discordant will and understanding in men is "a pure,
strong, and morally regulated love."[36] A morally perfected
character is one in which all divisions and distractions of the
four faculties have been surmounted in the inner harmony of
love. This is a poetic and high-minded philosophy of self-
perfection, in which will is characterized by the central act
of love.

A similar, but today more influential, reaction to abstract
Hegelianism is found in the writings of the Danish, religious
existentialist, Søren Kierkegaard. He opposes rationalism and
intellectualism in early nineteenth-century philosophy of religion (which he blames on Hegel) and tries to substitute for
this system-building a philosophy of love. The very title of a
book published by Kierkegaard, in 1847, tells a story: it is
called, *Purity of Heart Is to Will One Thing.*[37] He admits that
will is a "center from which choice springs,"[38] but insists that
choice is not the most distinctive act of willing. The man
faced with an intellectual choice between alternatives is ironically dubbed the "double-minded man," the person who is
always hesitating and failing to act. "The double-minded
man," Kierkegaard maintains, "stands pondering and reflect-
ing. If he is wholly absorbed in his pondering, then he continues to stand—a symbol of double-mindedness."[39] In a sense,
Kierkegaard is restating the position of Augustine and Anselm, when he says that man's supreme freedom and greatest

use of his will consists in loving one thing above all else, the Good.[40] This primary object of human willing is, of course, God.

In contemporary existentialism, some thinkers have parted company with Kierkegaard and gone the way of atheism. Perhaps Gabriel Marcel is today the most authentically Christian representative of the school. In his *Mystery of Being*, Marcel frequently criticizes the abstractness of academic philosophy. He argues that the distinction of will from intelligence "is really quite superficial. A will without intelligence would be a mere impulse, and an intelligence which lacked will would be devitalized."[41] Marcel further urges the importance of keeping "affectivity" united with intelligence and will. The mainspring of anti-theism, according to Marcel, "is the will that God should not be."[42] This is why he has no great confidence in "proofs" for the existence of God: they carry no conviction with people who display "a kind of fundamental ill-will which is basically pride."[43] Doubtless Marcel considers that the bent of man's will and love has a great deal to do with what he understands. On this point, as on many others, he has exerted an influence on Jacques Maritain. The theme of connatural knowledge, an understanding rooted in affectivity, has been central in many of Maritain's recent works.[44]

In the United States, during the early eighteenth century, Jonathan Edwards took an intellectualist position on the human will. He is not a philosopher who stresses love and affection. In some ways, Edwards is not far removed from the psychology of Thomas Aquinas. His *Treatise concerning Religious Affections* is more concerned with understanding and intellectually-guided willing than with what we would today recognize as affection or feeling. Yet he does make room for higher religious emotions, as the following text indicates:

God has endowed the soul with two faculties: one is that by which it is capable of perception and speculation, or by which it discerns, and views, and judges of things; which is called *understanding*. The other faculty is that by which the soul does not merely perceive and view things, but is inclined with respect to the things it views or considers; either is inclined to them, or is disinclined and averse from them; or is the faculty by which the soul does not behold things, as an indifferent unaffected spectator, but as either liking or disliking, pleased or displeased, approving or rejecting. This faculty is called by various names; it is sometimes called the *inclination;* and as it has respect to the actions that are determined and governed by it, it is called the *will:* and the mind, with regard to the exercises of this faculty is often called the *heart.* . . . And, it is to be noted, that they are these more vigorous and sensible exercises of this faculty that are called the *affections.*[45]

Notice that Edwards grants but two higher faculties to man, intelligence and will, and he makes religious affection or love a function of will.

To this, the nineteenth-century Faculty Psychologists objected strongly. Albert Bledsoe flatly contradicted Edwards, in a book published in 1845, at Philadelphia:

The truth is, [wrote Bledsoe] that in feeling the mind is passive; and it is absurd to make a passive impression the active cause of anything. The sensibility does not *act*, it merely *suffers*. The appetites and passions, which have always been called the "active powers," the "moving principles," and so forth, should be called the passive susceptibilities . . . the will [is] the *active power.*[46]

Bledsoe then defends "free will" against what he regards as the volitional determinism of Edwards, by affirming that there is introspective evidence of three distinct powers in man:

We are merely conscious of the existence of *thought*, of *feeling*, of *volition* . . . from the fact of consciousness that we do act, or put forth volitions, we are forced, by a fundamental law of belief, to yield to the conviction that we are free.[47]

Asa Burton, the founder of this school of psychology, called the three faculties: understanding, heart and will.[48] The understanding knows, the heart undergoes feelings, and the will acts. Frequently, Burton uses the term, taste, for the heart or faculty of sensibility. As he explains it:

Taste is the subject operated upon, when objects afford us either pleasure or pain. The understanding is not the subject on which they operate: for that has perceptions, but not emotions; it is a perceiving, but not a feeling faculty.[49]

Volitions, operations of the will, are actions which are carried out in movements of the body. "The immediate object of volition is generally the motion of the whole body, or some one of its members."[50] Feeling (when strong is called passion, when gradual and abiding it is called affection), is the source or "spring" of volitional activity. As Burton sums up the teaching: "The will is only an executive faculty. It is no more than a servant to the heart, to execute its pleasure. The will is no primary principle of action; its office is to obey the commands of the heart."[51]

Thus, at the end of our survey of people who regard love or affection as the typical activity of will, we find a group of thinkers who continue to regard such feelings as the ultimate, inner source of personal activity, but they transfer these affections to a new faculty and make the will its servant. This is, indeed, an odd development.

Throughout the earlier history of philosophy, "heart" is more or less identified with will, especially when love is taken as a central type of volitional function. Love, of course, is understood as affective approval of a known or felt object. It goes without saying that the contrary feeling, hate, is also taken as a typical and central movement of will in such a theory. Where will is taken as the "faculty of love," other volitional functions, such as desire, intention and choice, are usually made peripheral.

Catholic devotional practice and literature provide a special instance of the use of the heart-language in reference to the love of God. The "Sacred Heart" of Jesus is regarded as the rather concrete embodiment of the love of Christ for mankind. In extension, this view is sometimes also applied to the Mother of Christ, in the expression, "the Sacred Heart of Mary." While this usage has a deep religious significance, I do not find that it entails any new notion of volition, other than the emphasis on love which we have already noted.

NOTES

1. Claude Tresmontant, *A Study of Hebrew Thought*, trans. M. F. Gibson (New York: Desclée Co., 1960), pp. 119, 121.

2. Tresmontant, *op. cit.*, (pp. 125–131) cites Exodus 7:13; Judges 8:14; Isaias 10:7, 12; 41:22; Job 7:17, 20.

3. St. Paul, Romans 10:1 and 9–10; see also verses 6 and 8.

4. Werner Jaeger, *Diokles von Karystos* (Berlin, 1938), pp. 50–51.

5. Cf. G. Verbeke, *L'Evolution de la doctrine du Pneuma* (Louvain-Paris: Desclée de Brouwer, 1945), p. 13.

6. On Aristotle, see Jaeger, *op. cit.*, p. 50.

7. *Ibid.*, p. 219; see also Verbeke, *op. cit.*, *p.* 15.

8. St. Augustine, *Confessiones,* I, 1.

9. *De Trinitate,* XV, 21, 41: "voluntatem nostram vel amorem seu dilectionem quae valentior est voluntas."

10. Saadia Gaon (ben Joseph), *The Book of Beliefs and Opinions,* trans. from the Arabic and the Hebrew, by S. Rosenblatt (New Haven: Yale University Press, 1948). The original is entitled: *Kitâb al Amânât (Sepher ha-Emunoth we-ha-Deoth).*

11. Rosenblatt trans., pp. 243–244.

12. *Ibid.,* p. 245: "the human soul . . . its seat is in the heart."

13. Bahya ibn Pakuda, *Duties of the Heart,* ed. with the Hebrew trans. by Judah ibn Tibbon and English trans. by Moses Hyamson, 5 vols. (New York, 1925–1947). The citation is from vol. V, p. 27.

14. See Simon of Tournai, *Disputationes,* 51, 3 (ed. J. Warichez Louvain: Specilegium Sacrum Lovaniense, 1932); and Alanus ab Insulis, *Regulae de sacra theologia,* 79; *PL* 210, 661–662.

15. St. Thomas summarizes this twelfth-century view of the affective and effective wills, in his *Q.D. de Veritate,* XXIII, 1, in obj. 6.

16. Cf. E. Gilson, *History of Christian Philosophy in the Middle Ages,* p. 702; citing *AHMA* X–XI (1936), 334–335.

17. St. Bonaventure, *In II Sent.,* d. 39, 2, 1, c: "necesse est ponere quod synderesis se teneat ex parte affectus . . . sic synderesis non nominat illud pondus voluntatis, sive voluntatem cum illo pondere, nisi inquantum illam habet inclinare ad bonum honestum."

18. K. Michalski, "Le Problème de la volonté à Oxford et à Paris au XIVe siècle," *Studia Philosophica,* II (1937), 233–365. This publication was made available to me through the courtesy of the Yale University Library.

19. *Ibid.,* pp. 275–279.

20. St. Bonaventure, *In II Sent.,* 25, 1, 6, ad 2m. For a full study of Bonaventure's theory of love, see: Z. Alszeghy, *Grundformen der Liebe. Die Theorie der Gottesliebe bei den hl. Bonaventura* (Rome: Gregorianum, 1946).

21. Guillelmi de Valle Rouillonis, O.F.M., *Liber de Anima,* ed. Ignatius Brady, O.F.M., in *Mediaeval Studies,* X (1948), 225–296; XI (1949), 247–300.

22. *Q.D. de Virtutibus in communi,* art. 5, c. et ad 5m: "charity is in the will."

23. *In III Sent.,* 27, 2, 2, resp. (Both texts are fully cited in my *Pocket Aquinas,* New York: Washington Square Press, 1960, pp. 215–216, 364.) Of the many secondary studies of the Thomistic theory of love, the following are recommended: D'Arcy, M.C., *The Mind and Heart of Love* (New York: Holt, 1947); Geiger,

L.B., *Le Problème de l'amour chez saint Thomas d'Aquin* (Paris: Vrin, 1952). (Vs. Rousselot, next item.)

Rousselot, P., "Pour l'histoire du problème de l'amour au moyen-âge," *BGPM*, V, 7–102.

Simonin, H. D., "Autour de la solution thomiste du problème de l'amour," *AHMA*, VI (1931), 174–276. (The basic study.)

Stevens, Gregory, "The Disinterested Love of God according to St. Thomas and Some of his Modern Interpreters," *Thomist*, XVI (1953), 307–333, 497–541.

24. *Troilus and Cressida*, Act II, scene 2, lines 163–173.

25. T. Hobbes, *Elements of Law*, I, 7, 1–2 (ed. F. Tönnies, Cambridge: University Press, 1928, pp. 21–22).

26. J. Locke, *Essay concerning Human Understanding*, Bk. II, 21, 73.

27. G. Berkeley, *A Treatise concerning the Principles of Human Knowledge*, Part I, c. 27 (Everyman ed., 1925, p. 126.)

28. D. Hume, *A Treatise of Human Nature*, II, 3, 1 (ed. Selby-Bigge, p. 399).

29. For many uses of the heart-language, see: *Hume Selections*, ed. C. W. Hendel (New York: Scribner, 1927), pp. 197, 205, 208, 242, 394.

30. *An Enquiry concerning the Principles of Morals*, sect. 1 (in Hendel's *Selections*, p. 197).

31. A. Bain, *The Emotions and the Will* (New York: Appleton, 1888), p. 303.

32. *Ibid.*, p. 313; for a similar explanation, see Bain's *Mental and Moral Science* (London: Longmans, Green, 1868), p. 2.

33. J. J. Rousseau, *Emile*, trans. Barbara Foxley (New York: Dutton, 1948), p. 252.

34. F. von Schlegel, *Philosophy of Life*, trans. A. J. W. Morrison (London: Bohn, 1847); my quotation is from a selection in Robinson, *Anthology of Modern Philosophy* (New York: Crowell, 1931), p. 511.

35. *Ibid.*, in Robinson, p. 517.

36. *Ibid.*, p. 520.

37. S. Kierkegaard, *Purity of Heart Is to Will One Thing*, trans. D. V. Steere (New York: Harper Torchbooks, 1956).

38. *The Journals of Kierkegaard*, trans. A. Dru (New York: Harper Torchbooks, 1959), pp. 44–45.

39. *Purity of Heart*, p. 74.

40. *Ibid.*, p. 54.

41. G. Marcel, *The Mystery of Being* (Chicago: Regnery, 1951), p. 178.

42. *Ibid.*, p. 176.

43. *Ibid.*, p. 175.

44. See in particular, J. Maritain, *Approaches to God*, trans. by P. O'Reilly (New York: Harper, 1954); and *Neufs Leçons sur les notions premières de la philosophie morale* (Paris: Téqui, 1951).

45. J. Edwards, *A Treatise concerning Religious Affections*, (Boston 1746), in *The Works of J. Edwards*, ed. Perry Miller (New Haven: Yale University Press, 1957–1959), vol. II (1959), p. 99.

46. A. T. Bledsoe, *An Examination of President Edwards' Enquiry into the Freedom of the Will* (Philadelphia, 1845), pp. 101–102; the passage is cited in Schneider, *History of American Philosophy*, p. 236.

47. Bledsoe, *id.*, pp. 229–230; italics added by present writer.

48. A. Burton, *Essays on Some of the First Principles of Metaphysicks, Ethicks, and Theology* (Portland: Arthur Shirley, 1824), p. 18.

49. *Ibid.*, p. 54.

50. *Ibid.*, p. 85.

51. *Ibid.*, p. 91. The connection between this theory of will and the "executive will" of Alexander Bain, in England, is not clear. Bain's publications postdated those of the Americans.

The Will of the People

THE EXPRESSION, "will of the people," is much used in the literature of modern philosophy, politics and social thought. Other related phrases are: the general, popular, public or collective will. The usage is rarely defined in contemporary writings. Obviously, some power or action of volition is attributed to a human group but whether this means the unified function of a collectivity or the statistical preponderance of many individual volitions—this is not always clear. The latter possibility involves the difficult notion of the will of the majority, or "weightier part," of the citizens in a state. We propose to examine the development of this notion of will, in philosophical literature, in order to see whether it constitutes a meaning distinct from those which we have already examined.

Ancient philosophers do not seem to speak of this popular will. One might expect to find it in Plato, because one of the dominant themes in his *Republic* is the parallelism between the "parts" of the individual human soul and the classes in the Greek state. The ruling class, for instance, corresponds to the rational part of the soul. However, no part of the Platonic soul is will (*boulesis*) and it never occurs to Plato to attribute such a function to a group.

Cicero is the source of a widely quoted definition of a "people" (*populus*) in the political sense. "A people," he wrote, "is not just any gathering together of a multitude but a group joined together by their agreement to what is right and to their mutual advantage."[1] There is no mention of will, in this statement, but a volitional function is implied in the expression "by their agreement" (*consensu*). So far as can be determined, Cicero never mentions a *voluntas populi*, however.

St. Augustine cites this Ciceronian definition with approval.[2] He analyzes it and points out that it is most important for a people to love justice.[3] This is a function of will; consenting is a type of volition.[4] Finally, he maintains that the people of the City of God are united in their mutual love of divine justice.[5] Here we have all the elements of one version of the "will of the people" theme but Augustine does not call it that.

The middle ages knew of this Ciceronian-Augustinian definition of a people. It is simplified in Aquinas' statement that "a people is a multitude of men gathered under some end-directed relationship."[6] The full Ciceronian definition is accurately quoted, via St. Augustine, in a later passage in the *Summa of Theology*.[7] St. Thomas proceeds to explain how the functioning of political authority implies a certain acceptance of the governing power by the wills of the individual citizens.

Hence, it is pertinent to the meaning of a people that the mutual agreement of men be directed to the just precepts of law. Now there are two kinds of mutual agreements among men. One comes about by the authority of the ruler; the other is accomplished by the proper will [*propria voluntate*] of private persons. And since the fact of personal submission to a ruling power is a matter under the disposition of each man's will, therefore it must be by the authority of the rulers (to whom men are subject) that judicial sentences are carried out among men and punishments are inflicted on evildoers.[8]

Thomas Aquinas does not use the expression, will of the people, nor is his thinking on the subject directed to the notion of a general or group will, in the corporate sense in which we shall see this concept in modern philosophy. There is one sentence in his treatise, *On Kingship,* in which he speaks of the antipathy of most people to tyrants and adds: "what is against the *wishes of the multitude* cannot be long preserved."[9] This is as close as he came to the language of group volition. Some modern Thomists, of course, give the impression that Aquinas talked about the will of the people[10] but they can cite no texts that contain this sort of language.

It is possible that some ecclesiastical writers in the field of canon law who supported the Conciliar Theory thought in terms of the general will of all the members of the Catholic Church, even as early as the thirteenth century.[11] The concept and the terminology are clearly present in the following passage from Marsilius of Padua's fourteenth-century treatise.

Let us say, then, in accordance with the truth and counsel of Aristotle in the *Politics,* Book III, ch. 6 [1281a39ff] that the legislator, or the primary and proper efficient cause of the law, is the people or the whole body of citizens, or the weightier part thereof, through its election or will expressed by words in the general assembly of the citizens, commanding or determining that something be done or omitted with regard to human civil acts, under a temporal pain or punishment.[12]

As Gewirth says, "the people's will is the supreme efficient cause of all the institutions of the Marsilian state."[13] Marsilius does not offer much explanation of the will of the people

but it is obviously a type of group will which is sovereign
in the civil order (as opposed to the ecclesiastical) and
which is presumed to be directed to the common benefit of
the state and its citizens.[14] In this view, that the popular will
is nearly always right, Marsilius is anticipating an important
tenet of Rousseau concerning the general will.[15]

Another late medieval movement which has been interpreted
as using the concept of the will of the people is the
"translation theory" of political authority. From the late
thirteenth century onward, some Catholic writers have maintained that, although God is the ultimate source of the authority of all legitimate governments, the actual power to
rule is conferred on a given ruler or government by the
consent, election, or will of the citizens who originally
make up the body politic. Rommen summarizes the Suarezian
version of this theory, as follows:

As the will of those uniting for political life to perfect human
social nature and to live the good life in the *ordo justitiae legalis*,
is the cause of the state's coming into existence, the will of the
people is the cause of the transfer of authority from itself to a
king or anybody else. In other words, the constituent power is
actually with the people and of the people.[16]

This theory does not have to imply any notion of a single
"will" of the citizens as a corporate group. It may simply
mean that people have the power to elect their rulers.
This democratic interpretation is suggested by the way in
which St. Robert Bellarmine expresses the position at the
end of the sixteenth century:

Men must be governed by someone, lest they be willing to per-
ish. It depends upon the consent of the multitude to constitute

over itself a king, consul, or other magistrate. This power is indeed by the counsel and election of men. For legitimate reasons the people can change the government to an aristocracy or a democracy.[17]

It was a commonplace in early Jesuit writings to maintain, in opposition to divine right theorists, that the people make or select their own kings. This was the view that Suarez strongly defended against James I of England.[18]

It was not much more than a century later that Jean Jacques Rousseau proposed his theory of the general will. In his writings, the will of the people theme appears in its pure form and seems to constitute a new concept of volition. Briefly, Rousseau seems to have thought that, besides the individual wills of the men who make up the state, there is a higher will of the whole people. This he calls the "general will" and he assigns special properties to it.

First of all, let us see what Rousseau meant by the will of the individual man. Like Descartes, he considers man to be a union of two different substances, mind and body. Unlike Descartes, Rousseau takes it that his mind does move his body and that bodily sensations affect his soul. How such psycho-physical interaction is possible is a mystery and Rousseau admits that he cannot explain it.[19] However, man's will moves his body, and thus, Rousseau accepts the dynamic power meaning of will, which we have examined. Besides action, the function of choosing is most frequently assigned to the "particular" will, which is simply the volition of the individual man.[20] A well developed personality, according to Rousseau, acts and makes his choices in accord with the "voice of reason" and is not carried away by his passions.

It is well known that Rousseau felt that each man's nature

is basically good and that moral and social evils are due to a failure to adhere to the original simplicity and innocence which are man's endowments at birth. Indeed, this is the theme of the novel, *Emile*. He often speaks of two inborn principles or instinctive drives (also called dictates of the heart) which are prior to reasoning and which urge man in the direction of good activity.

Meditating on the first and simplest operations of the human soul, I think that I perceive two principles prior to reason, one of which makes us intensely concerned about our well-being and personal self-preservation, and the other inspires us with a natural repugnance to seeing any other being that is capable of feeling, and especially those of our own species, die or suffer.[21]

These instinctive tendencies toward the good of self and that of other persons are the bases for natural rightness, both in personal morality and in social intercourse. With these instincts, each person is able to live in association with his fellows. He will live well and develop his capacities, provided human society does not curb his good instincts by externally imposed and unnatural restraints in the form of arbitrary laws and social institutions. Rousseau's notion of the perfectibility of human nature includes not only a capacity for self-improvement in the individual person but also a similar factor in the human species.[22] Already present in this conception of the perfectibility of mankind as a corporate unity is the conviction that a group of men may have a power or function of the group—which is higher than the sum of their individual capacities.

It is but another step to the general will. In the *Discourse on Political Economy* which is a companion piece to the

Social Contract, the conditions for each man's entry into civil society are thus described:

Each one of us groups his person and his capacity under the supreme direction of the general will; and we take in each later member as an indivisible part of the whole.[23]

Every citizen in Rousseau's ideal state retains some of his own preferences, of course; individual wills still operate. These volitions are not always initially in accord with the corporate will of the people. However, individual differences tend to cancel out, leaving the over-all tendencies and decisions of the general will as the right and true will of all the citizens. Continued disagreement of the will of the individual citizen with the general will is impossible, in theory at least, since the corporate will is the expression of what is reasonable for the group, individually and collectively.[24] This is why the general will is infallible and always right.

When a decision contrary to my own wins out, that proves nothing more than that I was mistaken, and that what I thought to be the general will was not it. If my particular view had won out, I should have done something different from what I had really willed; in that case, I should not have been free.[25]

Rousseau shows a supreme confidence in the reasonableness and rectitude of this general will. It is something mystical to him, as Harald Höffding has commented.[26] Though merely expressed by the vote of the majority,[27] it appears to take on some of the attributes of divinity. We have seen that it is presumed to be infallible. In the Fourth Book of the *Social Contract*, the general will is described as indestructible, incorruptible, always constant, inalterable and pure.[28] This is not to say that the general will is always triumphant in the practical order of politics. Sometimes evil decisions sway the state—but Rousseau's point is that the general will *should* be followed in all cases. It invariably indicates what is in the interest of the citizen group, taken both collectively and distributively.

This is no ordinary meaning of will. Rousseau's general will is a power or function of a corporate group—and it is the essential principle of unity, action and decision for the ideal society of men which was intended to achieve heaven here on earth. So understood, the will of the people theory is in the background of later German notions on community will —and, in another context, of the democratic theory of majority rule.

It is in the violent reaction to Rousseau's theory and its apparent influence on the French Revolution that we may begin to appreciate the scope of this meaning of will. Edmund Burke is the leading spokesman of this critical reaction. He flatly contradicted Rousseau's claim that the general will is always right.

I see [wrote Burke] as little of policy or utility, as there is of right, in laying down a principle that a majority of men, told by the head, are to be considered as "the people," and that as such their will is to be law.[29]

Burke ridicules the idea that many men, voting in a group, are more likely to be right than one, or a few, men of wisdom. It was with this in mind that he wrote his often quoted and vitriolic lines on democracy:

But where popular authority is absolute and unrestrained, the people have an infinitely greater, because a far better founded, confidence in their own power. . . . The share of infamy that is likely to fall to the lot of each individual in public acts is small indeed. . . . Their own approbation of their own acts has to them the appearance of a public judgment in their favor. A perfect democracy is therefore the most shameless thing in the world. . . . It is therefore of infinite importance that they should not be suffered to imagine that their will, any more than that of kings, is the standard of right and wrong.[30]

Edmund Burke did not believe in the infallibility of the will of the people.

Indeed, few British writers have. John Stuart Mill, often regarded as an apostle of democratic liberties, is actually quite conservative concerning the meaning of the will of the people. For him, it stands for the power of those men (and they may be few) who actually achieve political authority.

The 'people' who exercise the power are not always the same with those over whom it is exercised; and the 'self-government' spoken of is not the government of each by himself, but of each by all the rest. The will of the people, moreover, practically means the will of the most numerous or the most active part of the people, the majority, or those who succeed in making themselves accepted as the majority.[31]

L. T. Hobhouse is much closer to an appreciation of the general will, when he argues that political liberty does not mean that each man may follow his own will but simply that it, "guarantees that his will is to count among the rest in making the decisions, and that the community as a whole will be bound by the main current of will flowing within it."[32]

Modern German philosophy offers many versions of the general will. It is well known that Kant was much impressed by Rousseau's political and practical views. In a sense the Rational Will of Kant's ethics is a principle higher than the mere elective preferences of the individual man. This *Wille* transcends the interests of the person and indicates the laws of universally good moral activity. To this extent, Rousseau has influenced Kant.

Fichte's description of the "common will" is actually much closer to the doctrine of the social contract and, of course, quite open to the mystique of the historical destiny of the German people. His *Addresses to the German Nation* (1807–1808) were a romantic call to the Germans to adopt a general will which would enable them to take their place as leaders in world history.[33] His meaning of the common will is spelled out in the *Science of Rights.*

As a will, that which we seek must have itself for its own object and its own perfection as its ultimate object. The commonwealth is the very harmony of all. Thus the commonwealth is the will we seek and as will wills itself which is the harmony of all. The common will then is the private will of this power. This harmony, the commonwealth, passes out of the realm of mere conception inasmuch as the will of some certain number of men in some particular time-moment becomes really harmonious and declares itself as such, thus entering the realm of the science of rights.

The common will must be established as the unchangeable and permanent will of all, which each agrees to recognize so long as he remains in the commonwealth; a fact which must always be borne in mind. The whole future will of each individual will is concentrated into the one moment when he declares his willingness to form the state.[34]

There is some sort of relation between this will of the state and the Infinite Will which Fichte lauds as a sort of apotheosis of his own personality.

Sublime and Living Will! named by no name, compassed by no thought! I may well raise my soul to Thee, for Thou and I are not divided. Thy voice sounds in me, mine resounds in Thee; and all my thoughts, if they be good and true, live in Thee also.[35]

The full sense of this lyrical passage is not at all clear but obviously Fichte uses the term, will, to designate some sort of higher and transcendent principle. Earlier in the same text, he speaks of this eternal will as "Creator of the World." It is well to remember that, in Fichte's subjective idealism, he makes the world for himself. The text is more than an essay in egotism, however, because Fichte really means that the individual volition of the person is able to pass over into some sort of will of the community.

Hegel also talks at great length about the common will of the citizens of a state. His *Philosophy of History* suggests that the state results from the combination of the subjective (individualized) will with the rational will.[36] However, this does not necessarily mean a type of group volition. The universal will of Hegel is more like a projection of the will of the individual man into an order which transcends his individuality.[37]

The will is then universal, because all restriction and all particular individuality have been absorbed within it. These lie only in the difference between the concept and its content or object, or, to put it otherwise, in the difference between its implicit character and its subjective awareness of itself, or between its universality and its exclusive individuality, the individuality which resolves.[38]

In National Socialism, under Hitler's guidance, the "Fuehrer principle" maintained that the leader personifies the will of the people. Nazi propagandists, such as Alfred Rosenberg and Joseph Goebbels, went back to Fichte's political writings to find philosophical justification for their totalitarian and racist theories.[39] Jacques Maritain blames the rise of totalitarianism on a perverted interpretation of the will of the people. He speaks of this unfortunate version of the popular will as,

reducing the community to an atomized mass of individuals confronted with an all-powerful State in which the will of each one was supposed to engulf and annihilate itself and mystically come to life again in the form of the general will.[40]

This indicates one variation of meaning that has been given to the group will in the twentieth century.

Maritain himself uses the expression "will of the people" in the context of democratic institutions and seems to mean by it the actual decisions of the majority. He insists that this "will" is not sovereign, in the sense that Rousseau gave to it, and also that it is not the source of justice.[41] In fact, most writers on democracy occasionally mention the "will of the people"; it is an accepted phrase in contemporary political philosophy and such usage hardly needs documentation here.

What the expression actually means today, in the United States, is not so easy to say. It is a good phrase, with a resounding quality that fits well into most any political speech. Certainly, very few Americans would understand it as the "general will" of Rousseau, or as the "common will" of Fichte. It has recently been suggested that it means little more than public opinion.

The product of advertising, we are told, is 'consumer demand.' And what is that but public opinion or the will of the people? In making us see the 'will of the people' as a version of consumer 'demand, popular sovereignty as consumer sovereignty, the marketplace view of life strikes a fundamental blow at the conception of self-government.[42]

The same writer, Joseph Tussman, suggests that the will of the people is extremely inarticulate and difficult to discover in a modern democracy. He compares the work of the public official who tries to determine the will of the people to the role of the architect who makes the plan of a house from the vague hints of his client.[43] The present meaning of the term is indeed nebulous.

Efforts have been made, in recent philosophical writing, to give a more definite meaning to the notion of the popular will. In one sense, Mortimer Adler's two volumes, *The Idea of Freedom*, are directed to this purpose. His chapters on political and collective liberty[44] are particularly pertinent to the present topic. As long as freedom is taken as the mere absence of restraints external to the agent, however, such investigations can contribute little to the understanding of the volitional processes of the individual or the group.

Natural law thinkers try to give some substantive meaning to the popular will by associating it with the concept of a common good for human society and right reasoning concerning the means used for the attainment of such a good. As Maritain remarks, "The will of the people is not sovereign in the vicious sense that whatever would please the people would have the force of law. The right of the people to govern themselves proceeds from natural law. . . ."[45] Of course, this means practically nothing, if philosophers and legal theorists take it that all law emanates from the fiat of a sovereign will.[46] We shall consider this theory of the legislative will, in the next chapter.

In quite another philosophical context, Brand Blanshard has recently proposed a theory of the "real and rational will" which is reminiscent of the *Wille* of Kant but which, in effect, maintains that both personal and community endeavors require some ideal conception of a highest good at which men may aim. Volition is irrational without some rational goal. Blanshard's argument is well worth considering.

The real will goes beyond the actual will; it does so everywhere and always. That is the point of the contrast between them. The good that would completely satisfy me is never achieved in this act or that. To recognize the real will is to arouse discontent with what is, to indict the good I have actually achieved in the light of what might be. To say, in the *individual* case, that the recognition of the real will meant somehow glorifying the actual would be so patently contrary to the point of the distinction as to wear its falsity on its face. How is the case different when we turn to the will of a community? The recognition of a real will is the recognition that there is a greatest good for that community and that it is the business of the citizens to regulate their communal life so that this good may be as fully embodied as possible. The very insistence on the distinction implies that one is ordinarily to obey the law, but, as we have seen, one cannot so much as state the reason for that obedience without acknowledging an authority above the law, which we may invoke against the law itself if that should fail.[47]

Blanshard sees the state (which is constituted by the will to community) as a "contrivance" that men need in order to realize their common end. His explanation of this helps to summarize much of what is most thoughtful in the practical aspirations of Western man. Blanshard states it in four propositions.

First, we can distinguish within our own minds between the end of our actual or immediate will, and the end of our rational will, which is what on reflection would commend itself as the greatest good. Secondly, this rational end is the same for all men. Thirdly, this end, because a common end, is the basis of our rights against each other. Fourthly, the justification of the state, and its true office, lie in furthering the realization of this end.[48]

Of course this is an expression of an ideal, of moral and political idealism, but what is the will of the people without some such idealism?

At the end of this chapter on the will of the people, it must be admitted that, although the usage is very common in modern works on political philosophy, the meaning of the popular will is not entirely distinct from the notions of personal volition that have been presented in the preceding chapters. Efforts to erect a theory of group volition as the characteristic activity of a state or organized society are not convincing. They do not introduce a new meaning into our understanding of will. If the state is personified, as it is in some German versions of the theory, then its will is simply a larger—but not qualitatively different—instance of personal volition. If, on the other hand, the will of the people is understood as but a more extensive use of rational choice or appetite, then this meaning has been seen already.

Taken as the elective activity of a political group, the will of the people is much more than a metaphor, of course. It is an important factor in political sovereignty. The popular will is clearly a significant element in the development of democratic institutions. Just as clearly, the tyrant or the dictator may claim to embody in his personal decisions the will of the people whom he controls. Without some sort of real or rational directions, the popular will is a will-o'-the-wisp.

NOTES

1. M. T. Cicero, *De Re Publica*, I, 25; the Latin and English texts may be read in the translation by C. W. Keyes (Loeb Classical Library), Cambridge, Mass.: Harvard University Press, 1952: "Populum autem non omnem coetum multitudinis, sed coetum iuris consensu et utilitatis communione sociatum esse determinat." (The English quotation is my own literal version.)

2. St. Augustine, *De civitate Dei*, II, 21; for the English, see: *City of God* (New York: Doubleday Image Books, 1958), p. 73.

3. *Ibid.*, XIX, 21; Image ed., p. 469.

4. *Ibid.*, XIV, 6: "Nam quid est cupiditas et laetitia, nisi voluntas in eorum consensionem quae volumus?" Cf. Image ed., p. 303.

5. *Ibid.*, XIV, 28; Image ed., pp. 321–322.

6. St. Thomas, *Summa Theologiae*, I, 31, 1, ad 2: "populus enim est multitudo hominum sub aliquo ordine comprehensorum."

7. *Ibid.*, I–II, 105, 2, c: "sicut Augustinus in II De civitate Dei introducit a Tullio dictum, 'populus est coetus multitudinis iuris consensu et utilitatis communione sociatus.'"

8. *Ibid.*, the key phrase in Latin is: "quia voluntate uniuscuiusque disponi protest quod eius subditur potestati"; this is mistranslated in the usual English versions.

9. St. Thomas, *De Regno*, I, 10: "non potest enim diu conservari quod *votis multorum* repugnat." The translation is from: *On Kingship*, trans. Phelan-Eschmann (Toronto: Pontifical Institute of Mediaeval Studies, 1949), p. 46. (Italics have been added.)

10. See "general will" and "will of the people" in: T. Gilby, *The Political Thought of Thomas Aquinas* (Chicago: University of Chicago Press, 1958), pp. 199, 259–260, 299.

11. Thus Gilby, *op. cit.*, p. 200: "The concept of authority responsive to some kind of general will lay deep in the Canonical Tradition. . . ." He cites Brian Tierney, *Foundations of the Conciliar Theory: The Contributions of the Medieval Canonists from Gratian to the Great Schism* (London: Cambridge University Press, 1955).

12. Marsilius of Padua, *The Defender of Peace*, vol. II: *The Defensor Pacis*, trans. with introd. by A. Gewirth (New York: Columbia University Press, 1956), Discourse One, ch. XII, p. 45.

13. *Ibid.*, vol. I: *Marsilius of Padua and Medieval Political Philosophy* (which is Gewirth's *Introduction*), 1951, pp. 60–61, and see p. 170.

14. *Ibid.*, vol. I, 58–59.

15. Cf. Rousseau, *Contrat social*, II, 3: "La volonté générale est toujours droite et tend toujours à l'utilité publique." This sentence is quoted by Gewirth, *op. cit.*, I, 58, note 34.

16. H. Rommen, *The State in Catholic Thought* (St. Louis: Herder, 1945), p. 449.

17. This text from Bellarmine is quoted in W. L. Willigan and J. J. O'Connor, *Social Order* (New York: Longmans, 1941), p. 24; I have been unable to locate it in Bellarmine's writings.

18. F. Suaresii, *Defensio Fidei*, I, 3, 3; *De Legibus*, I, 3, 4–5.

19. J. J. Rousseau, *Emile* (in *Oeuvres*, Paris: Lequien, 1821, IX, 27): "Il ne m'est pas plus possible de concevoir comment ma volonté meut mon corps, que comment mes sensations affectent mon âme. Je ne sais pas même pourquoi l'un de ces mystères a paru plus explicable que l'autre. Quant à moi, soit quand je suis passif, soit quand je suis actif, le moyen d'union des deux substances, me paroît absolument incompréhensible."

20. *Ibid.*, vol. IX, 29: "Agir, comparer, choisir sont les opérations d'un être actif et pensant."

21. Rousseau, *Contrat social* (*Oeuvres*, IV, 206).

22. Thus Rousseau speaks of a "faculté" which helps to develop all the other powers, "et réside parmi nous tant dans l'espèce que dans l'individu." *Ibid.*, vol. IV, 227.

23. Rousseau, *Discours* (*Oeuvres*, V, 112).

24. "En effet, s'il n'est pas impossible qu'une volonté particulière s'accorde sur quelque point avec la volonté générale, il est impossible au moins que cet accord soit durable et constant; car, la volonté particulière tend, par sa nature, aux préférences, et la volonté générale à l'égalité." *Ibid.*, V, 122.

25. *Ibid.*, V, 225–226.

26. Höffding, *Jean Jacques Rousseau and His Philosophy*, trans. W. Richards (New Haven: Yale University Press, 1930), pp. 133–134.

27. "Du calcul des voix, se tire la déclaration de la volonté générale." *Discours* (*Oeuvres*, V, 225).

28. *Contrat social*, IV, 1; cf. *Discours* (*Oeuvres*, V, 22): "S'ensuit-il de là que la volonté générale soit anéantie ou corrompue? Non: elle est toujours constante, inaltérable et pure. . . ."

29. Burke's comment is quoted in: A. Castell, *Introduction to Modern Philosophy* (New York: Macmillan, 1943), p. 428.

30. E. Burke, *Writings and Speeches* (Boston: Little, Brown and Co., 1901), vol. III, 354–355.

31. J. S. Mill, *On Liberty*, ch. I; in *Utilitarianism, Liberty, and Representative Government* (New York: Dutton, 1944), p. 68.

32. L. T. Hobhouse, *The Elements of Social Justice* (London: Allen and Unwin, 1949), p. 88.

33. J. G. Fichte, *Addresses to the German Nation*, trans. R. F. Jones and G. H. Turnbull (Chicago: Open Court, 1922).

34. *Science of Rights*, trans. A. E. Kroeger (London: Trübner, 1889), p. 208.

35. *Vocation of Man*, ed. Chisholm, p. 139, *op. cit.*

36. G. W. F. Hegel, *Philosophie der Geschichte (Sämtliche Werke*, ed. M. Glockner, Stuttgart: Fromann Verlag, 1927–1939, vol. XI, 69–70): "Dieses Wesentliche ist selbst die Vereinigung des subjektiven und des vernünftigen Willens: es ist das sittliche Ganze— der *Staat* . . ." See: *Philosophy of History*, trans. Sibree, p. 38.

37. Cf. W. T. Stace, *The Philosophy of Hegel* (New York: Macmillan, 1924), pp. 321 ff.

38. Hegel, *Philosophie des Rechts (Werke*, VII, 30–31).

39. See my article, "The Philosophical Antecendents of German National Socialism," *Thought*, XIV (1939), 225–242, which refers to Rosenberg's *Der Mythus des 20 Jahrhunderts* and Goebbels' *Wesen und Gestalt des Nationalsozialismus*.

40. J. Maritain, *Christianity and Democracy* (New York: Scribner, 1944), p. 72.

41. Maritain, *Man and the State* (Chicago: University of Chicago Press, 1951), p. 48.

42. J. Tussman, *Obligation and the Body Politic* (New York: Oxford University Press, 1960), pp. 111–112.

43. *Ibid.*, pp. 97–98.

44. Adler, *The Idea of Freedom*, vol. I (1958), chapters 18–19, pp. 329–399; for a bibliography of other group publications on the concept of freedom, *ibid.*, pp. 652–658.

45. *Man and the State*, p. 48.

46. Cf. V. J. Bourke, "Two Approaches to Natural Law," *Natural Law Forum*, I (1956), 92–96.

47. B. Blanshard, *Reason and Goodness* (London: Allen and Unwin; New York: Macmillan, 1961), p. 404.

48. *Ibid.*, p. 397.

CHAPTER VIII

Will as the Source of Law

THE THEORY that will in some way produces law is found in many medieval and modern philosophers. It involves a special way of looking at law and, as a consequence, a highly distinctive notion of will itself. Law is understood as implying a strong note of obligation. The subjects of law are considered to be bound by a fiat of the legislator's will to do certain actions and to omit other actions. In this theory, what makes a law to be in full force is the fact that the lawmaker formally intends or wills that the subjects must obey the commands of his law. The legislator *may* indicate that the law is to be obeyed by assigning certain rewards and/or punishments to the law. But such sanctions are not necessary to all forms of this theory. We shall see that Scholastic penal law thinkers insist that sanctioning is important to the enforcement of law and that the assigning of a penalty indicates to the subjects that the lawmaker expects the law to be broken at times and merely wills that the subjects be ready to accept the penalty in case of infractions. On the other hand, Kant supports a theory of legislative will, in which sanctions have nothing to do with the essential obligation of the law.

For our study, what is significant in the general theory of the legislative will is the view that will is a dominant factor in human psychology. In the case of a theologian who maintains that the divine will is the supreme source of law, he regards will as a supreme attribute of God. Indeed, people who make will, either divine or human, the source of law nearly always assign certain cognitive functions to will. They suggest that will orders, regulates, commands, and prescribes modes of appropriate action. They insist that will foresees the results of compliance and non-compliance with its edicts, and that will judges legal and illegal conduct, assigns rewards and punishments (if these are provided), and that will is even able to see when exceptions are to be made. If one readily grants that all these functions are clearly within the competence of the lawmaker's will, then he is a legal voluntarist. If, however, a person thinks that the foregoing functions are mainly the work of intellect rather than of will, then he could be termed a legal intellectualist. We are concerned in this chapter with legal voluntarism.

Ancient philosophy, to my knowledge, offers no example of the theory of legislative will. The Greeks and the Romans exalted reason (*logos, ratio*) and maintained that a good, orderly life is that which is lived in accord with reason. Consequently, ancient thought sees law as an expression of what is reasonable in the field of action. Cicero illustrates this non-volitional view of law:

For the soul admits of a twofold division, one of which partakes of reason, the other is without it; when, therefore, we are ordered to give a law to ourselves, the meaning is that reason should restrain our rashness. There is in the soul of every man something naturally soft, low, enervated in a manner and languid. Were there nothing besides this, men would be the greatest of monsters; but there is present to every man reason, which presides over and gives laws to all; which, by improving itself, and making advances, becomes perfect virtue. It behooves a man, then, to take care that reason shall have command over that part which is bound to practise obedience.[1]

This Ciceronian explanation of the origin of law would seem to give no role to will. In the thirteenth century, Thomas Aquinas (who knows Cicero very well[2]) will take it that reason means intellect, or one of its functions, and will speak of law as an "ordinance of reason," not of will.[3] On this point, St. Thomas is in full agreement with his teacher, Albert the Great, and he will be followed by key theologians at the beginning of the modern era. Cajetan, Soto, Medina and Bellarmine maintain that the act of commanding (*imperium*) is an intellectual function and does not essentially pertain to will. As a consequence, this group of thinkers does not hold that will is legislative.[4]

Other Scholastic writers, practically contemporary with the foregoing men, take the opposite view. Starting in the last quarter of the thirteenth century and running down into modern times, are many prominent and influential Catholic thinkers who insist that to order or command action is primarily the work of will. Leading men in this school are Henry of Ghent, Duns Scotus, William of Ockham, Gabriel Biel, Alfonso de Castro and Francisco Suarez. These thinkers do not say that reason is excluded from the legislative function. They all admit that "right reasoning" has something to do with the establishment and proper functioning of law. However, they assign to intellect a fringe activity in the work of ordering or commanding activity and they insist that will is the central faculty in the making of law.

William of Ockham is one of the more extreme members of this school. There is little doubt that he considers the will the most important power in the human soul and that volition dominates intellection in the functioning of man's soul.[5] Moreover, Ockham so stresses the omnipotence of divine will that he resents any suggestion that there are any limitations of reason on what God may will, and will rightly. As he puts it: "God cannot be obligated in regard to any act; and so, by the very fact that God wills it, this is the just thing to be done."[6] Ockham admits that there is a conformity between every right act of will and right reason but he hastens to add that this does not mean that right reasoning always precedes right willing and shows what should be willed. Instead, "by the very fact that the divine will wills it, right reason dictates that it is to be willed."[7]

For Ockham, the human will is essentially free in all its activities. Man's will is a power of self-determination which constitutes the essence of human personality.[8] Like the Greek *hegemonikon*, Ockham's will is the "boss" of all the other powers of the human soul. This implies that will is in no way subject to direction or dictation from intellect. In no sense is the human will passive; it is a completely active potency.

Actually, this view goes gack to Duns Scotus and before him to certain late thirteenth-century thinkers. In 1270 and 1277, Etienne Tempier had condemned a number of teachings on will which he regarded as erroneous. He was the Bishop of Paris at this time and he was concerned about the religious effects of such doctrines in his diocese. Some of these condemned teachings can be identified with the views of Andreas Capellanus and the writings of the "courtly love" school.[9] Here are some of the condemned theses:

a) That the soul wills nothing, unless moved by another. Whence this is false: the soul wills itself. An error, if moved by another means by the appetible or the object, in such a way that the appetible or the object is the total reason for the movement of this will.

b) That the appetite, when impediments are removed, is necessarily moved by the object of appetition. An error in reference to the intellective [appetite].

c) That the will of man is necessitated by his cognition, as is the appetite of a brute.[10]

Bishop Tempier is obviously favoring a notion of human will that is foreign to, or even critical of, the psychology of Thomas Aquinas. Tempier had been a professor at the University of Paris and his philosophic position may be described as a traditional Augustinianism, in which will is entirely free and active. Soon, other critics of St. Thomas are found who take up the Bishop's lead and oppose the Thomistic teaching that the human will is a partly passive potency, subject to intellectual regulation and not free in all its acts. Approximately in the year 1278, William de la Mare is writing that Aquinas is quite wrong in saying that the act of commanding belongs to reason, and that reason is the cause of liberty. William is a strong defender of the primacy of will.[11] Another man with similar views, in the late thirteenth century, is Walter of Bruges who supports the radical independence of the human will.[12] In the same years, Peter John Olivi says that the intellect depends on the will for the sublimity of its understanding: without this volitional guidance, the human intellect could not, at least on such a high level, see the truth.[13] Olivi argues that we can directly experience within our consciousness the will moving itself to action and the complete volitional control of the other human functions. "To say that our act of willing (*velle*) is not the highest commanding function (*actus summe imperiosus*) is manifestly opposed to our inner experience," says Olivi, "for we sense its commanding control (*imperiositatem*) most clearly and intimately."[14]

It is in such psychologies of volition that it makes sense to attribute the origin of law to will. William de la Mare, Walter of Bruges and Olivi are Franciscan theologians. Their approach to will culminates in the partial legal voluntarism of

Duns Scotus and the fully developed theory of the legislative will in William of Ockham, which we have mentioned earlier. Although Duns Scotus is not a complete voluntarist (for he sees some need of right reasoning in conjunction with the proper activities of the human will), he does in fact think that all specifically human actions are to be attributed to the faculty of will. In a key section of his *Prologue* to the definitive edition of his *Commentary on the Sentences*, [15] Scotus discusses the character of human action in the moral area. He argues that such action, for which he uses the Greek word *praxis*, is nothing but an elicited or commanded act of will: "praxis ad quam extenditur habitus practicus non est nisi actus voluntatis elicitus vel imperatus." Notice what this means: all human actions are either *elicited* (begun and completed within the power of will), or they are *commanded* (begun within the will and completed in other human potencies that are ordered or directed in their activities by the will). Obviously, the act of commanding (*imperium*) is no longer regarded as the function of intellect: to command now means to will. It is but one further step to the conclusion that to make law is to will.

That the theory of the legislative will is no isolated phenomenon of a minor branch of Scholasticism becomes clear when we look at the work of Francis Suarez. Teaching and writing at the end of the sixteenth and the beginning of the seventeenth centuries, Suarez is but two centuries removed from the theologians whose views we have just examined. He read Thomas Aquinas, Duns Scotus, William of Ockham and many other philosophers and theologians. In his *Disputationes Metaphysicae*, Suarez cites the views of two hundred previous writers. His *Treatise on Laws* (*De Legibus*) is likewise a vast compendium of the literature of legal thought. Suarez was a law student before he entered the Society of Jesus and he maintained his interest in jurisprudence throughout his life. Although he regarded himself as a Thomist, it is clear that the psychology and legal philosophy of Suarez are not, and cannot be, mere repetitions of the thought of Thomas Aquinas. If we think of Thomism, Scotism and Ockhamism as the three points of a triangle, then we may picture Suarezianism as a type of thought which falls within this triangle, on some questions moving closer to one point, on others approaching a different point. To some readers it looks like eclecticism but Suarezianism is a well informed and highly personal philosophy which shares some of the features of all the major schools of earlier Scholasticism with systematic consistency and coherence. Certainly, on the problem of the relation of will and law, Suarez differs from Thomas Aquinas.

Let us start our examination of the Suarezian teaching by quoting the general definition of law. According to Suarez, law is "an act of a just and right will by which a superior wills to obligate his inferior to do this or that."[16] Here we may note two points: law issues from the will of the legislator; and obligation is an essential and central factor in the meaning of law. God, in making the supreme law, freely decrees with the divine will to bind creatures to obey it.[17] In the case of human laws, they derive their obligatoriness, their binding force, from the will of the human lawmaker.[18] The act of commanding, both divine and human, is the function of will and not of intellect.[19] For Suarez, the legislative will cannot be purely arbitrary or irrational in its decrees. On this point, he is much closer to Duns Scotus than to Ockham. He speaks very favorably of the importance of right reasoning, as explained by Aquinas, but when the chips are down Suarez opts for the supremacy of will in the legislative process. He insists that the human intellect is not a commanding or ordering power; the understanding intimates or declares what is right or wrong but it remains for the will actively to require and direct what is to be done.[20] No doubt remains that Suarez is, in a cautious and guarded way, a legal voluntarist.[21]

What sort of will does this Suarezian theory imply? Let us confine our brief discussion to the human will. First of all, Suarez speaks of will as rational appetite but he agrees with Scotus and Ockham that freedom is the generic characteristic of all volition. This freedom of will is unconditioned and is a liberty of indifference.[22] This means that the human will always retains, even in the very exercise of its action, the active power to cease or modify its activity. Of course, Suarez is here but following the decision of the Council of Trent which, in the middle of the sixteenth century, had decreed that liberty lies in the power of indifference.[23]

Secondly, willing is now explained almost wholly in terms of efficient causality. Where Thomas Aquinas had assigned an important role to the end or good toward which the appetite tends, Suarez now treats this causality of the end as a metaphor.[24] Historically, this represents the outcome of a continuing trend in Scholasticism, from the fourteenth century onward, to minimize the importance of final causes and to emphasize efficient causality. For Suarez, the human will needs neither formal nor final causes to specify it or to bring it into a state of peak activity. As he explains, "the appetitive power (i.e. will) is of itself in first act . . . of itself it is inclined toward the good; hence it needs no form by which it might be established in first act."[25]

From this time on, the Thomistic theory of intellectual appetite is no longer the typical teaching of Scholastic philosophy and theology. Some modified version of the Scotistic-Suarezian will becomes the common teaching of the textbooks.

St. Francis de Sales shows how far removed we are from Thomas Aquinas, when he flatly states:

Among the numberless multitudes and varieties of actions, movements, sentiments, inclinations, habits, faculties and powers that are in man, God has established a natural monarchy, and it is the will that commands and dominates over all that is found in this little world.[26]

Mercier's *Psychology* (a textbook still in use in the twentieth century) quotes the foregoing description of will (which is reminiscent of the Stoic hegemonikon) with full approval.

When John Locke studied philosophy at Oxford, he learned this theory of will from Scholastic textbooks, some of them written by Catholics, some by Protestant scholars in the Low Countries and Germany. In 1954, Locke's *Essays on the Law of Nature* were published for the first time.[27] They show that as a young writer Locke was a thorough legal voluntarist. He speaks of law as the declaration of the will of the legislator.[28] Like Suarez, Locke makes obligation essential to law and cannot conceive of a law which does not stem from will, either human or divine.[29] In his later works, Locke speaks of the law of nature as the law of reason[30] but British philosophy continues to think of law as the work of will. William Paley, in the eighteenth century, speaks like a Protestant Suarezian. The will of God determines right and wrong and the divine will is known to us in two ways: (1) as revealed in Scripture; (2) through the "light of nature." Paley explains that obligation is always associated with "the idea of a command, an authority, a law, a will."[31]

Immanuel Kant is the most prominent modern philosopher to assign a legislative function to will. It is well known that he introduced the terminology of "legislative will" in discussing the Categorical Imperative. Kant tried to find some rule which would neatly enable a person to distinguish between moral right and wrong. The solution to his quest was the Categorical Imperative which he states in three ways:

I. Act only on that principle which thou canst will should become a universal law.
II. Act as if the principle of thy action were to become, by thy will, a universal law of nature.
III. So act as to treat humanity, whether in thine own person or in the person of another, as an end withal, never as a means only.[32]

Notice that "will" is used in the first two versions but does not occur in the third, as quoted. However, the sentence immediately preceding the third formula is: "From this as a supreme practical law, all laws of the will must be capable of being deduced." So it is quite clear that will plays a central role in all of Kant's treatments of his Imperative. Actually he insists on, "the idea of the will of every rational being as a universally legislative will."[33] The problem of the interpreter is to discover what Kant meant by will in such a context. Let us start with a key text:

Appetition is the faculty of being by means of one's ideas the cause of the objects of these ideas. . . . The appetitive faculty which depends on concepts, in so far as the ground of its determination to action is found in itself, not in the object, is called a faculty of *doing or forbearing as we please*. In so far as it is combined with the consciousness of the power of its action to produce its object, it is called elective will (*Willkuehr*); if it is not so combined, its act is called a wish. The appetitive faculty whose inner determining principle, and consequently, even its 'good pleasure' (*Belieben*), is found in the reason of the subject, is called the Rational Will (*Wille*). Accordingly, the Rational Will is the appetitive faculty, not (like the elective will) in relation to the action, but rather in relation to what determines the elective will to action; and it has itself, properly speaking, no determining ground; but in so far as it can determine the elective will, it is practical reason itself. That which is determinable only by inclination would be animal will. Human elective will, on the contrary, is one which is *affected*, but not *determined*, by impulses. It is accordingly in itself (apart from acquired practice of reason) not pure; but it can be determined to action by pure will. Freedom of the elective will is just that independence of determination by sensible impulses. This is the negative concept of it; the positive is: the power of pure reason to be of itself practical.[34]

A good part of Kant's explanation of volition is present in this text. Rational will (*der Wille*) is practical reason. In its pure form this practical reason is not subject to anything else; in particular, it is not sullied by sensory experience. Pure practical reason is not a blank tablet, like the understanding in John Locke; it has its inner resources of practical guidance. It is will as identical with practical reason that is the legislative source of moral law. We should not take this to mean that Kant thought that each man could arbitrarily decide for himself what moral laws he might choose to obey. Kant was a very strict and high-minded moralist. Arbitrariness is not good will. In one sense, he agreed with the later Scholastics who insisted that will must be the total cause of its acts. But Kant pushed this thesis to the point of claiming that a proper will must be the source of the very principles in terms of which it operates. To do something for a reason that is other than a will-reason, this is to abandon will in its essence and to act upon some lower impulse. We can see what Kant is trying to do: he is keeping will as a faculty of moral action but is do-

ing this at the expense of expanding will to take in some of
the functions which a man like Thomas Aquinas would attribute to a distinct faculty of intellect. Kant puts it this way:

Everything in nature works according to laws. Only a rational
being has the capacity of acting according to the conception of
laws, i.e., according to principles. This capacity is will. Since
reason is required for the derivation of actions from laws, will is
nothing else than practical reason. If reason infallibly determines
the will, the actions which such a being recognizes as objectively
necessary are also subjectively necessary. That is, the will is a
faculty of choosing only that which reason, independently of
inclination, recognizes as practically necessary, i.e., good.[35]

How, then, do we know what is good and endeavor to will
it, on a level superior to the private and possibly base inclinations and impulses of the moment? That is what Kant tried
to answer in the theory of the Categorical Imperative. He is
thinking about a will that has some connection with Rousseau's general will. This point has been very ably developed
in a recent book by Brand Blanshard which is not, of course,
an exposition of Kant's theory of will but which rethinks the
problem in terms of what Blanshard calls the "real and rational will."[36] He suggests at one point that "we can distinguish within our own minds between the end of our actual
or immediate will, and the end of the rational will, which is
what on reflection would commend itself as the greatest
good."[37] Later on, Blanshard has a sentence which might have
been written by Kant:

Rationality, as we conceive it, does not lie merely in letting reason
appoint one's beliefs, hard as that is; it means carrying a rational
spirit into the ramifications of practice, making it permeate one's
feelings and pervade all the decisions of one's will.[38]

I am inclined to think that this sums up the main point that Kant has made in his theory of the legislative will. It may be an incomplete one but it is not a bad doctrine.

During the nineteenth and twentieth centuries one very influential type of jurisprudence has been that which has come to be called legal positivism. This name has no connection with our contemporary philosophical school of logical or scientific "positivism." In legal philosophy, positivism designates the view that all law is *positive*, that is, it results from an act by which a sovereign legislator places, or puts forth, a commanding regulation under the formal conditions of legislative authority. Such a jurisprudence looks to no more ultimate source, or criterion of validity, for law than the duly exercised will of the legislator. Justice is what the existing law of a state says it is. For the legal positivist, it is nonsense to appeal to any higher or more ultimate standard of rightness. Neither the law of God, nor the law of nature, nor the traditional customs of mankind (in the sense of a *Jus Gentium*) has anything to say about justice. Justice is always what the legislature and the courts now will it to be.

In British jurisprudence, John Austin (1790–1859) was a key representative of voluntaristic positivism.[39] As far as he is concerned, the just is merely that which is in accord with a statute or a court decision. Austin's views and their apparent consequences are summed up as follows, by F. C. S. Northrop:

Law, according to Austin, is identified with the commands or will of the sovereign, where this will is indivisible and legally unlimited. It follows that legal sovereignty cannot be divided between the executive, legislative and judicial branches of government, but must be located completely in one of them. In a society, therefore, whose living law is monarchical, this definition of law requires the placing of the whole of the government's sovereignty in the executive branch, i.e., an absolute monarch. In a society where living law is democratic, it necessitates similarly that the whole of political sovereignty must be placed in the legislative branch. From this, three things follow: (1) The executive becomes merely the spokesman for, and executive officer of, the majority in the legislature. This is the case in Great Britain and in Free India. (2) The judiciary becomes merely the instrument for taking the will of the legislature as expressed in its statutes as the sole meaning of law and for applying this purely statutory positive law to the settling of disputes; all previous judicial decisions, if scientifically correct, being such applications of the legislature's absolute and legally unlimited will. Hence, the epoch-making effect upon recent American politics and United States Supreme Court decisions of the British positivistic philosophy of law which came into this country through Thayer.

Austin's legal positivism has one other consequence. Since it equates the whole of law with a sovereign will which is legally unlimited, thereby restricting, in a democratic society, the tasks of advocates and judges to the application of the legislative statutes to concrete cases, it follows that (3) the subject matter of legal science is nothing but the positive law.[40]

We may observe how necessary to legal positivism is the acceptance of a sovereign will which is governed by, and grounded in, nothing but itself. This appears to be the apotheosis of will in the politico-social order. Impossible to describe or analyze such a will; it is unlimited and unconditioned, subject to no restrictions save those which it may choose to set up, and to change at its pleasure, for its own sovereign functioning.

Legal positivism, then, leaves no room for a philosophy of law. Why bother with any jurisprudence, when the sovereign will neither requires nor can brook such theoretical guidance? More than this, the thorough-going legal positivist can see no need for any kind of philosophy, theology, or science. When the sovereign will of the government in Soviet Russia declares that a certain biological theory is unacceptable, its decision is final (at least for the time being) and science must conform. Most British and American exponents of the view do not go this far, it is true, but that is because they retain some respect for the traditional, non-positivistic ideals of freedom of thought and of professional and scientific integrity.

Let us finally examine one kind of modern Protestant theology in which the will of God is not the source of law but is itself the only law of goodness and rightness. There has been in this field of theology a decided reaction against intellectual, rational, conceptual system-building. To many contemporary Protestant theologians, the older philosophies of religion now appear but empty abstractions which must be rejected. Kierkegaard's critique of Hegelianism set the pattern for this anti-rational reaction. All that is necessary is for the individual person to submit his will to the sovereign Will of God. In some types of contemporary religious existentialism, "commitment" is a cardinal act. One must make a basic, personal decision, an act of willing to accept God or to reject Him. St. Augustine had said it, long ago, in the *City of God*: there are only two kinds of people, those who are with God and those who are against Him. It is idle to speculate about the divine attributes, to attempt to reason out the rules of ethical living, to erect vast edifices of doctrine. Such conceptualization has nothing to do with salvation.

As Reinhold Niebuhr states the position, in his Gifford lectures: "No pattern of human reason but only the will of God can be the principle of the form and order to which human life must be conformed."[41] It would seem that this is a religious voluntarism in which a notion of human willing is present, a view of will which bears some resemblance to the legislative will. Instead of saying that the divine will decrees certain universal patterns of conduct which men may come to know with their understandings and accept with their wills, Reinhold Niebuhr seems to do away with the need for law by insisting that the good Christian will be ever ready to accept the immediate and personal promptings of the Will of God. Universality drops out of the picture. Every good act is a volitional relationship to the divine will. The whole religious personality becomes a series of fitting volitions. There have always been Christians who have maintained that philosophy and theology are irrelevant to salvation, who have seen no need for faith to seek understanding. Niebuhr is not far from St. Bernard of Clairvaux, when he writes in the twentieth century:

To understand himself truly means to begin with a faith that he is understood from beyond himself, that he is known and loved of God and must find himself in terms of obedience to the Divine Will.[42]

In conclusion, what is generally characteristic of this theory of the legislative will? It appears that will becomes that faculty, power, or aspect of human or divine nature whereby right order, and so goodness, are produced by virtue of an authority, or sovereignty, which admits of no superior standard. Whatever edict such a will issues is *ipso facto* legal and right. The law is what the legislator wills. In this view of will, the act of commanding is central and distinctive. Such an understanding of will can culminate in a very high-minded ethics and political philosophy. It can also end in the sophistries of penal law thinking, in the rejection of all permanent codes of human conduct, in the superficiality of legal positivism, and even in the kind of nonsense that once was dignified by the name National Socialism and is now known in another totalitarian guise as Soviet jurisprudence.

NOTES

1. M. T. Cicero, *Disp. Tusc.*, II, 21; in *The Academic Questions, Treatise de Finibus, and Tusculan Disputations*, trans. C. D. Yonge (London: Bohn, 1853), p. 356.

2. Cf. E. K. Rand, *Cicero in the Courtroom of St. Thomas Aquinas* (Milwaukee: Marquette University Press, 1946).

3. *Summa Theoligiae*, I–II, 90, art. 1–4.

4. For the views of both the intellectualist and voluntarist groups, see: T. E. Davitt, *The Nature of Law* (St. Louis: Herder, 1951).

5. Speaking of Ockham, Ueberweg-Geyer, *Geschichte der scholastischen Philosophie* (Berlin: Mittler, 1928), p. 581, puts it bluntly: "Der Wille besitzt dem Verstand gegenüber die Superiorität."

6. "Deus autem ad nullum actum potest obligari; et ideo eo ipso quod Deus vult, hoc est justum fieri." Ockham, *In IV Sent.*, q. 9 E.

7. "Omnis voluntas recta est conformis rationi rectae sed non est semper conformis rationi rectae praeviae quae ostendat causam quare voluntas debet hoc velle. Sed eo ipso quod voluntas divina hoc vult, ratio recta dictat quod est volendum." *In 1 Sent.*, d. 41, q. 1 K.

8. See D. J. B. Hawkins, *A Sketch of Medieval Philosophy* (London: Sheed & Ward, 1946), p. 118.

9. A. Denomy, "The *De amore* of Andreas Capellanus and the Condemnation of 1277," *Mediaeval Studies*, VIII (1946), 107–149.

10. These are nos. 194, 134, and 159, in the numbering of the *Chartularium Universitatis Parisiensis* (Paris, 1889), vol. I, 553.

11. For these views in the *Correctorium Corruptorii "Quare,"* see the critical ed. by P. Glorieux in *Les premières polémiques thomistes* (Kain: Le Saulchoir, 1927), I, pp. 409–410; and the comment in H. de Lubac, *Surnaturel* (Paris: Aubier, 1946), pp. 267 ff.

12. E. Longpré, (ed.) *Quaestiones disputatae du B. Gauthier de Bruges* (Louvain, 1928), pp. 39–61; see the analysis in Gilson, *History of Christian Philosophy*, p. 688.

13. "Videtur mihi quod intellectus ex eo quod est unitus voluntati

sortitur tam in modo existendi quam in modo aspiciendi objecta sua quandam sublimitatem et quoddam regimen sine quo non posset, saltem ita alte, veritatem speculari." Peter J. Olivi, *Quaestiones in II Sent.*, q. 57; ed. Quaracchi, 1926, vol. II, 331.

14. "Dicere quod nostrum velle non sit actus summe imperiosus est manifeste contra nostrum sensum internum, quia eius imperiositatem nos expressissime et intimissime sentimus." *Ibid.*, vol. II, 332.

15. J. D. Scotus, *Ordinatio*, Prologo, pars V, q. 1 (Quid sit praxis), in *Opera Omnia* (Civitas Vaticana: Typis Polyglottis Vaticanis, 1950), tome I, pp. 156–159.

16. Suarez, *De Legibus*, I, 5, 24 (*Opera Omnia*, Paris: Vivès, 1856–1878, V, 22).

17. *Ibid.*, II, 3, 9 (tome V, 94).

18. *Ibid.*, II, 4, 8 (tome V, 99).

19. *Ibid.*, I, 4, 11 (tome V, 16).

20. See the analysis by Davitt, *op. cit.*, ch. VI, pp. 86–108.

21. For two views on legal voluntarism in Suarez, see: J. de Blic, "Le volontarisme juridique chez Suarez," *Revue de Philosophie*, n.s. 10 (1930), 213–230; and E. Jombart, "Le volontarisme de la loi d'après Suarez," *Nouvelle Revue Théologique*, 59 (1932), 34–44. For Suarez' early views: J. Giers, *Die Gerechtigkeitslehre des Jungen Suarez*, Edition und Untersuchung seiner Römischen Vorlesungen *De Iustitia et Iure* (Freiburg: Herder, 1958).

22. "Sit ergo primum hujus materiae fundamentum certissimum dari in nobis talem libertatem quale in ipso usu humanorum actuum indifferentiam . . . habeat . . . quod ipse usus sit cum indifferentia quam retinet potentia etiam in ipso instanti in quo libere operatur." *Opusculum Primum*: *De Concursu motione et auxilio Dei*, c. 1, n. 8.

23. For the decree of the Council of Trent (A.D. 1545–1563), Sess. 6, can. 5, see: Denziger-Bannwart-Umberg, *Enchiridion Symbolorum* (Romae, 1937), nn. 814–815; cf. n. 797.

24. Suarez, *De Anima*, V, 3, 8.

25. "Potentia appetitiva de se inclinatur ad bonum, proindeque nulla eget forma per quam in actu primo constituatur." *De Anima*, V, 3, 5.

26. The citation of St. Francis de Sales is given without reference in: D. Mercier, *La Psychologie*, 7me éd. (Louvain-Paris: Institut Supérieur et Alcan, 1905), pp. 228, note 1.

27. J. Locke, *Essays on the Law of Nature*, ed. W. von Leyden (New York: Oxford University Press, 1954).

28. *Idem.*, p. 184.

29. Cf. M. B. Crowe, "Intellect and Will in John Locke's Con-

ception of the Natural Law," *Atti del XII Congresso Internazionale di Filosofia* (Firenze, 1960), vol. XII, 129–135.

30. *Second Treatise of Civil Government,* ch. II, 6 and 11; cf. Crowe, *art. cit.,* p. 134.

31. For an analysis of these points in Paley's *Principle of Moral and Political Philosophy* (1785), see: Castell, *Introduction to Modern Philosophy,* pp. 288–297.

32. Kant, *Foundations of the Metaphysics of Morals,* II; ed. L. W. Beck (Chicago: University of Chicago Press, 1949), pp. 80, 87; the *Critique of Practical Reason,* I, 1, 1, n. 7, offers a fourth formulation.

33. Kant, *Fundamental Principles of the Metaphysics of Morals,* trans. T. K. Abbot (New York: Liberal Arts Press, 1949), p. 49.

34. *Kant's Critique of Practical Reason and Other Works,* trans. T. K. Abbott (London: Longmans, 1954), pp. 281–283.

35. The passage is from Beck's version of the *Foundations of the Metaphysics of Morals,* ed. cit., p. 72.

36. B. Blanshard, *Reason and Goodness* (London: Allen and Unwin; New York: Macmillan, 1961), p. 394.

37. *Ibid.,* p. 397.

38. *Ibid.,* p. 409.

39. John Austin, *The Province of Jurisprudence Determined and the Uses of the Study of Jurisprudence,* ed. H. L. A. Hart (London: Oxford University Press, 1954); for the view that the just is simply what the legislature or the courts say it is, pp. 184, 260–261.

40. F. C. S. Northrop, "Philosophical Issues in Contemporary Law," *Natural Law Forum,* 2 (1957), 48–49.

41. Reinhold Niebuhr, *The Nature and Destiny of Man* (New York: Scribner, 1949), vol. I, 28.

42. *Ibid.,* p. 15.

CHAPTER IX

Will as Reality

DURING THE TWENTY-FIVE CENTURIES that have marked the course of Western philosophy and theology, there have been a number of thinkers who have maintained that will or volition is constitutive of reality. In effect, these people have suggested that *to be* is *to will*. Some of them have said that the divine will is the ultimate source of all things and that the universe and mankind share in the volitional character of this supreme will. Others simply take it that some sort of nondivine will constitutes the whole of things. Obviously, these views imply a special metaphysics which might be termed voluntarism.

Plato is not a metaphysical voluntarist but his description of the Ideal Form of the Good, as tending inevitably to share its goodness with other things, may be a remote antecedent of the claim that reality is volitional in character. Dialogues such as the *Republic* and the *Timaeus* suggest that the Good is diffusive of itself and thus constitutive of at least one aspect of the many things of this universe. However, the Idea of the Good is not an agent of the process of world-making; the Good is but an exemplary cause, and not the only one, in this process.

In the third century of the Christian era, Plotinus taught a modified type of Platonism in which he pictured all reality as a series of emanations from an original One. Plotinus' *Enneads* view the One as ineffable, beyond all being, goodness and other ordinary perfections. This initial Unity gives rise to an Understanding (*Nous*) of itself, a first pluralization of the One in which there is a duality of the knower and the thing known. A second emanation, that of Soul (*Psyche*), represents a further pluralization of things, culminating in the many realities of this universe. As a weak example, we might think of this in terms of a point (which stands for the original One); then, we might imagine this point expanding into a small circle (which would represent Intelligence); and finally, we could think of this little circle expanding into a much larger circle (which would symbolize Cosmic Soul). Beyond this larger circle is no other geometric figure; this absence of a figure could stand for matter. In the world of Plotinus, matter is a limit; matter is the complete lack of unity; matter is nothing. Man is described as a combination of a little piece, as it were, of cosmic soul with matter. Man lives on the borderline between the nothingness of the material and the unity of the immaterial. In this precarious state, man's soul may turn its attention downwards toward matter or upwards toward the One. If it chooses to concentrate on material things, the soul of the individual man becomes like them and terminates in nothing; it is annihilated. On the other hand, if a man's soul is turned up to the One, it more and more acquires the character of Unity and is thereby perfected. Throughout the fourth *Ennead*, Plotinus reviews various psychologies that have been developed by earlier Greek philosophers, by Plato, Aristotle and the Stoics. It is clear that he is interested in the nature of human willing, because the soul's act of turning its attention downward or upward seems to be a volitional one. He is particularly scornful of Stoic psychology, perhaps because of its basic materialism.

The last *Ennead* returns to the discussion of the One and,

in its Eighth Chapter, offers some insights on the freedom and will of the One.[1] Plotinus is somewhat dependent on Aristotle's treatment of the *hekousion* in the *Nicomachean Ethics*.[2] This is what has come to be called the "voluntary" in Latin and English commentaries on Aristotle. Plotinus connects this notion of voluntariness with will, using both Greek words, *thelesis* and *boulesis*.[3] He discusses what it means to be the master (*kyrios*) of one's actions and then applies the theory to the One, in the following text:

In the One, power (*dynamis*) is not open to contraries; it is an irresistible and immovable force, which is the greatest possible. . . . Who could change it, since it is generated from the divine will, and is His will (*boulesin ousan*) itself? . . . Will was, then, in His essence; in fact, it (*boulesis*) is nothing other than His essence. . . . He is entirely will; there is nothing in Him that does not will.[4]

It would seem legitimate to conclude that Plotinus is, here, at least hinting that the fundamental character of reality is some sort of volitional energy or force.

This metaphysics of will continues in the Neo-Platonic school, after Plotinus. Two centuries later, Marius Victorinus is converted to Christianity and he combines Plotinus' teaching with some theological notions (apparently distorted) concerning the second Person of the Trinity. At least one historian of philosophy, Benz, sees Victorinus as a key personality in the growth of a new theory of reality in which will is the central concept.[5] In his *Book on Divine Generation*, Victorinus vaguely suggests that the Word of God is the divine intelligence and will, which has emanated from the eternal will of God.[6]

There is a good deal of Mohammedan and Jewish speculation on the will of God, during the early middle ages. One Mohammedan sect, the *Ashariya* of the tenth century, held that the divine will holds together the discrete elements of space and time. Were this bonding influence of will to be withdrawn, all finite reality would fall into nothingness.[7] The eleventh-century Jewish thinker, Avicebron (Ibn Gabirol), also makes the will of God to be a unifying force throughout the universe. His main work, the *Fountain of Life* (*Mekor Hayim*), became very influential in a twelfth-century Latin translation by Dominic Gundissalinus and deserves special attention here.

Where Plotinus had described the successive emanations, or outpourings, of the many from the One as possibly the results of a supreme Will, Avicebron (writing eight centuries later and with a knowledge of the Jewish tradition) retains the concept of emanation but identifies its source and perhaps its material cause as the Will of God. As the *Fons Vitae* puts it:

To describe will is impossible; but an approximate description may be given, when we say that it is the divine power, making matter and form and binding them together, diffused from the highest to the lowest, like the diffusion of the soul in the body; and it is moving all things and disposing all.[8]

Now this is not a particularly surprising statement for a theist to make but Avicebron has his own peculiar understanding of the Will of God. This divine will is identical with God's essence, *when not acting*, but *when it is acting*, this divine will is considered a sort of first creature, an initial projection of energy and formal reality into creation. And so, as acting, the divine will is something distinct from the essence of God. Avicebron says: "the will which is His [God's] power is infused into everything and is penetrating everything, and nothing is without it, for both the being of all things and their very structure (*constitutio*) arise out of it."[9]

He is conscious of the fact that there is some background in the history of philosophy for his theory. The *Fons Vitae* takes it back to Greek philosophy, saying:

Plato [actually, it is Plotinus] thought that forms are made in the Intelligence by virtue of the attention of the Will, and they are next made in the universal Soul by virtue of the gaze of universal Intelligence, and they are likewise made in nature and in substance by virtue of the looking of the universal Soul upon nature.[10]

Solomon Munk first identified Ibn Gabirol (Avicebron) as a Jewish thinker, in an important study published in the middle of the nineteenth century.[11] Munk wrote, concerning the above quoted passage:

We should not be surprised to see Will playing a role in teachings attributed to Plato and the Neoplatonic thinkers. The Arabs [Avicebron wrote in Arabic] often trace back to Plato and other philosophers the speculations of their own modern theologians. Compare Sharastâni, *History of Religious and Philosophical Sects* (Arabic text, p. 289; German trans. by Haarbrucker, vol. II, 126-127). According to this author, Anaxagoras could not have considered the Will and the action (of God) as things existing by themselves and having a form essential to themselves, but as things that do not exist except in their objects, which means that they are but abstract ideas of things produced by the first efficient cause.[12]

Munk goes on to say that Avicebron's views on the divine will as constitutive of reality were strongly influenced by an

anonymous medieval treatise, called the *Theology of Aristotle*.[13] This strange book was, of course, not written by
Aristotle. When its Arabic original was published (in 1882),
it was claimed that the Latin Renaissance version (made by
Peter Nicholas Castellani de Faenza, 1517–1519) was not a
literal translation of the Arabic. Munk had used the Latin text
and Guttmann and others accused Munk of misinterpreting
the sources of Avicebron. However, in 1930, a Russian
scholar named Borisov published fragments of another Arabic
text of the *Theology of Aristotle*, which show that the Latin
version was accurate and that Solomon Munk was generally
right in his interpretation. Borisov later published an important study, in a Russian journal, on the voluntaristic philosophy of Avicebron.[14]

There is little question that Avicebron represents a high
point in the development of a medieval metaphysics of will.
Fusing various borrowings from the Biblical account of creation, Neo-Platonic emanationism, and later *Logos* doctrines,
he arrived at a view of will as a hypostasis, partly identical
with God and partly separated from Him. Will thus becomes
a sort of universal form which enters into the constitution of
the real.[15] Since the *Fons Vitae* was available in Latin in the
thirteenth century, it was widely read by Christians and was
recognized as the work of a theist but was not then identified
as a Jewish work. It strongly influenced some of the views of
Albert the Great and Thomas of York.[16]

Early modern philosophy offers some evidence of a similar
theory in some Christian philosophers. Descartes' philosophy
has been termed voluntaristic but it does not appear that he
ever maintained that the created world is constituted out of
the substance of a cosmic will. Some of his followers, however, came very close to saying that all created things have
no reality apart from the will of God. This may look like a

very pious teaching but it actually minimizes the power of
God by suggesting that the divine act of creation terminated
in no real product. The world of creation then becomes a
mirage.

Abbé Malebranche, toward the end of the seventeenth
century, wrote several books in which he used the language
of Cartesianism, and some of Descartes' own views, to show
that this universe and mankind are nothing but movements
within the divine will. He is also much indebted to St.
Augustine but he misinterprets and twists the significance of
the thought of the Bishop of Hippo. Malebranche's *Recherche
de la Vérité* begins with about eighty pages of texts quoted
from Augustine. Augustine had, of course, spoken frequently
of man's utter dependence on God but he had never suggested that man and his universe are unreal. Nicholas Malebranche soon makes it clear that he underestimates the reality
of this world.

It is necessary [Malebranche writes] to establish clearly . . . and
to prove that there is only one true cause, because there is only
one true God; that the power of everything proceeds only from
the will of God; and all natural causes are not true causes but
only occasional causes.[17]

Now, what this actually means is well brought out in
Malebranche's *Dialogues on Metaphysics and Religion.* Here
he explains: "The act of creation never ceases, the conservation of created things being on the part of God merely a con-
tinuous creation, merely an act of volition which persists and
operates without ceasing."[18] The mind is much more important to Malebranche than body, yet he insists that even bodies
are inoperative without the divine will. "The moving force
of a body is [he adds] therefore nothing but the activity of

God's will which conserves it successively in different places."[19] The same is true of the activities of the human mind: these are all but movements of the divine will. "In a word [Malebranche concludes], He has willed—He wills incessantly—that the modifications of the mind and those of the body shall be reciprocal."[20] This is Occasionalism with a vengeance; not only is there no causal interaction between mind and body, there is no real secondary causality among bodily events or among psychic events. Since Malebranche seems to think that reality is active, one may conclude that, for him, the very existence of mind and body is in the divine will. He never quite says this but implies it in passages such as the following:

You find yourself in the world, without any power, immovable as a rock, stupid, so to speak, as a log of wood. . . . What would you do in order merely to move the tip of your finger . . . unless God came to your aid, your efforts would be vain, the desires which you formed impotent. . . . It follows that, notwithstanding the conjunction of soul and body in whatever way it may please you to imagine it, you would be dead and inert if it were not for the fact that God wills to adapt his volitions to yours—His volitions, which are always effective, to your desires, which are always impotent.[21]

A similar view is presented by Arnold Geulincx, a Belgian contemporary of Malebranche. In his *Ethics*, this man compares the parallelism of man's mind and body to the synchronism of two clocks which appear to be interconnected but which correspond in their movements, simply because they are operated by the same clockmaker.[22] This is not, perhaps, a metaphysics of will but it reduces all finite causality to the sole cause that is efficacious, the will of God.

Post-Kantian German philosophy provides us with several examples of people who maintain that reality is basically a self-determining process. What is, is some type of will. F. W. Schelling, in his *System of Transcendental Idealism*, wrote:

How at once the objective world conforms itself to ideas in us, and ideas in us conform themselves to the objective world, it is impossible to conceive, unless there exists, between the two worlds—the ideal and the real—a preëstablished harmony. But this preëstablished harmony itself is not conceivable, unless the activity, whereby the objective world is produced, is originally identical with that which displays itself in volition, and *vice versa*.

Now it is undoubtedly a *productive* activity that displays itself in volition; all free action is productive and productive only with consciousness. If, then, we suppose, since the two activities are only one in principle, that the same activity which is productive *with* consciousness in free action, is productive *without* consciousness in the production of the world, this preëstablished harmony is a reality, and the contradiction is solved.[23]

Notice that we have here a man who still sees the problem in terms of the psycho-physical parallelism of Descartes and Malebranche. But where they rely on God's will to supply the explanation of their apparent interaction, Schelling now gives this role to a sort of cosmic, or universal, will. As Frank Thilly said of Schelling:

The absolute ground, or source, or root, of all things is creative energy, absolute will or ego, the one all-pervading world-spirit, in which everything dwells in potency and from which everything that is actual proceeds.[24]

A theistic divine will has given place to a pantheistic voluntarism.

Johann Gottlieb Fichte developed another kind of voluntarism. Starting within individual consciousness, he pointed out that I am aware of myself as a knower and willer and that I am also aware of what is known and willed. Thus, he distinguishes two phases of consciousness, the ego and the nonego. Though consciousness is subjective, it appears to contain an objective element. Knowledge is important but willing seems to Fichte to be a more real and active function. As the following selection indicates, he implies that his own will projects the sum total of reality:

The will is the efficient, living principle of the world of reason, as motion is the efficient, living principle of the world of sense. I stand in the center of two entirely opposite worlds: a visible world in which action is the only moving power; and an invisible and absolutely incomprehensible world, in which will is the ruling principle. I am one of the primitive forces of both these worlds. My will embraces both. This will is in itself a constituent element of the supersensual world; for, as I move my will by successive resolutions I move and change something in that world, throughout which my activity thus extends itself giving birth to new and ever enduring results which henceforth possess a real existence and need not be again produced. The will may break forth in a material act; and this act belongs to the world of sense and does there what it can do.[25]

Notice that this will, to which Fichte attributes all the contents of his experience, is his own personal will. Descartes had said, "I think, and so, I am"; now Fichte is saying, "I will, and so, not only I but the whole world exists and moves!" This is the ultimate position in subjective voluntarism. My will is the stuff of the universe. Let us examine one further text, to make certain that we are not overstating the case.

I would exercise my voluntary power freely, for the accomplishment of aims which I shall have freely adopted: and this will, as its ultimate ground can be determined by no higher, shall move and mold, first my own body and through it the surrounding world. My active powers shall be under the control of my will alone, and shall be set in motion by nothing else than by it. Thus it shall be. There shall be a Supreme Good in the spiritual world; I shall have the power to seek this with freedom until I find it, to acknowledge it as such when found, and it shall be my fault if I do not find it. This Supreme Good I shall will to know, merely because I will it; and if I will anything else instead of it, the fault shall be mine. My actions shall be the result of this will; without it I shall not act at all, since there shall be no other power over my actions but this will. Then, my powers determined by and subject to the dominion of my will, will effect the external world.[26]

Obviously, Fichte is quite serious. He really thinks that his own will constitutes the reality of all things. Hocking summed up the position very well, when he said: "Fichte took the essence of mind to be will: will must express itself in action: action means the forming of stuff, or the overcoming of obstacles."[27] What did will actually mean to Fichte? Initially, he seems to have understood the term as Kant did: will is the practical reason, considered as essentially active. As Fichte describes it: "The will is the living principle of reason—is itself reason, when purely and simply apprehended."[28] However, he extends the concept of will, first to designate all that is efficient and productive, and eventually to mean all that is. His system is a metaphysics of will.

The same cannot be said of the absolute idealism of Hegel. He did not think that will was as important and all-prevading as the Fichtean will. Yet there are passages in the more practi-

cal works of Hegel where we find a sort of dialectic of volition, leading to the Absolute. If the subjective will is taken as
the positive moment, and the non-subjective (and so, abstract)
will as negative, then the third step which cancels the first two
is the Ideal Good as Willed. Hegel puts it this way in his
Rechtsphilosophie:

The *Good* is the *Idea*, as the unity of the concept of the will and
of the particular will. It is realized freedom, the absolutely final
purpose of the world. . . .
   Thus *the Good* is the absolutely essential for the subjective
will, which has worth and dignity only in so far as, in its in-
sight and intent, it corresponds with the good. . . .
   Supplementary.—The will is not absolutely good, but can
only become the good that it is potentially, through its own
labor. So too, the good without the subjective element is only
an abstraction. The development of the Good contains three
stages: (1) The good for me the willing one, is particular will
and I know it as such. (2) We define the Good and develop its
particular characteristics. (3) We have the act of pointing out
definitely what is good as such, the particularity of the good as
infinite self-dependent subjectivity.[29]

Elsewhere, in his *Philosophy of History*, Hegel observes
that the sphere of will is the material in which the historical
dialectic takes place and culminates in the State. This would
appear to be another example of a volitional dialectic.

In human knowledge and volition, as its material element, Reason
attains positive existence. We have considered subjective volition where it has an object which is the truth and essence of a
reality, viz., where it constitutes a great world-historical passion.
As a subjective will, occupied with limited passions, it is dependent, and can gratify its desires only within the limits of this

dependence. But the subjective will has also a substantial life— a reality—in which it moves in the region of *essential* being, and has the essential itself as the object of its existence. This essential being is the union of the *subjective* with the *rational* Will: it is the moral Whole, the *State*, which is that form of reality in which the individual has and enjoys his freedom; but on the condition of his recognizing, believing in, and willing that which is common to the Whole.[30]

It is but a step from these various types of voluntaristic idealism to the world-view of Arthur Schopenhauer. He, also, maintains that the complete reality of the universe, and of man's existence, is basically of the nature of will. This is not the Will of God, nor the will of the individual person, but a primitive and original force which has neither purpose nor goodness in it. As one of Schopenhauer's editors has remarked:

The will of which the world (and most clearly the organic world, and hence, our own individual lives) is the expression is essentially a primordial, ungrounded force, and a blind one. . . . That this will is blind means only that it has no further end than the mere perpetuation of existence—and bare existence, contrasted with existing *for* something, is the essence of meaninglessness.[31]

This comment makes it immediately evident why Schopenhauer is a pessimist. Neither the world, nor man's life, has any ultimate goal or meaning. This is why Schopenhauer's ethics is ambiguous and betrays inner and unresolved tensions. It would seem advisable for man to accept and live in accord with the basic drives of cosmic will: this would be to follow the course of nature, and nature is will. Yet the primordial will is not good; it is evil, and a higher morality

appears to demand that we endeavor to transcend and deny
the urgency of the blind force of will. This latter is in no
sense the will of a benevolent Deity. Schopenhauer makes this
clear in one of his *Essays*:

But if we enter within, and therefore take in addition the *subjective* and the *moral* side, with its preponderance of want, suffering, and misery, of dissension, wickedness, infamy, and ab-
surdity, we soon become aware with horror that we have before
us anything but a theophany.[32]

Schopenhauer developed his metaphysics of will in a series
of lengthy works. The treatise, *Ueber den Willen in der
Natur*, sketches the history of a good many earlier theories of
will, in which Spinoza and the German idealists seem to im-
press Schopenhauer most, and then the work argues that
cosmic nature is nothing but the objectification of will activity.[33] His work entitled, *Die beiden Grundprobleme der
Ethik*, contains two essays which purport to show how will
manifests itself in the psychological and moral life of man.[34]
But the most important metaphysical work that he produced
was undoubtedly *Die Welt als Wille und Vorstellung*.[35] Here,
he endeavors to explain "the meaning for which we seek of
that world which is present to us only as our idea (*Vorstellung*)."[36] After criticizing a purely physical explanation of
the universe, Schopenhauer goes on:

But all this is not the case; indeed the answer to the riddle is
given to the subject of knowledge who appears as an individual,
and the answer is *will*. This and this alone gives him the key
to his own existence, reveals to him the significance, shows him
the inner mechanism of his being, of his action, of his movements. The body is given in two entirely different ways to the

subject of knowledge, who becomes an individual only through his identity with it. It is given as an idea in intelligent perception, as an object among objects and subject to the laws of objects. And it is given in quite a different way as that which is immediately known to every one, and is signified by the word *will*. Every true act of his will is also at once and without exception a movement of his body. The act of will and the movement of the body are not two different things objectively known, which the bond of causality unites; they do not stand in the relation of cause and effect; they are one and the same, but they are given in entirely different ways,—immediately, and again in perception for the understanding. The action of the body is nothing but the act of the will objectified, i.e., passed into perception. It will appear later that this is true of every movement of the body, not merely those which follow upon motives, but also involuntary movements which follow upon mere stimuli, and indeed, that the whole body is nothing but objectified will, i.e., will become idea.[37]

Very little comment is needed, on this long text. Schopenhauer is telling us that will is everything. If it helps to put the point in Kantian terms, then we might note that Schopenhauer later says that, "the will alone is a thing-in-itself."[38] So, though man and the universe appear to be many things, of variegated characteristics, fundamentally all these are but the appearances of one underlying reality, which is will.

One cannot describe this metaphysical will of Schopenhauer. To attempt description would be to translate will into its phenomenal aspects, into what it imperfectly seems to be rather than what it is. Will is the ineffable principle of reality.

Once one has read Schopenhauer, other and later proponents of metaphysical voluntarism seem rather pale figures.

Eduard von Hartmann further explores the concept of an unconscious will. To him, will as unconscious is "the immanent cause of every movement in animals, which is not produced reflectorially."[39] Conscious willing is the cause of preconceived action and follows upon reflection. "What then in the present work is denoted by the word 'Will' is no other than the same essential principle in both cases."[40] One could find similar tendencies toward psychological voluntarism among many of the German founders of experimental psychology, in the nineteenth century. To the extent that they had a philosophical view of the human psyche, both Fechner and Wundt regarded mental or spiritual activity as a manifestation of will. What they meant by will is not different from what we have seen in Schopenhauer.

The case of Friedrich Nietzsche is different. There is no doubt that will is a most important factor in his thought but there would be some question as to whether he has a metaphysics of will; this is because it is not clear that he had any metaphysics. James Collins remarks that Nietzsche "agrees with Schopenhauer that will constitutes the essential nature of the real, although the will is no longer a noumenal backdrop for Nietzsche, but is only the dynamic aspect of the 'appearances'."[41] Interpretation of Nietzsche is made more difficult by the way in which his sister, Elizabeth Foerster-Nietzsche, interfered with the content of his writings. *The Will to Power*, one of his most widely read books, was not written in that form by Friedrich Nietzsche but was a compilation by his sister of various selections from his other works and notes.[42] However, the notion of the *Wille zur Macht* is present in nearly all his writings and it is a quasi-universal principle of his philosophy. Unlike Schopenhauer, Nietzsche is convinced that the drive of universal will is a movement toward the morally approvable maximization of the human species. The "Superman" (*Uebermensch*) is what makes life worthwhile. We read in his book *On the Genealogy of Morals*:

Similarly, the evolution of a 'thing,' of a custom, is anything but its *progressus* to an end, still less a logical and direct *progressus* attained with the minimum expenditure of energy and cost: it is rather the succession of processes of subjugation, more or less profound, more or less mutually independent, which operate on the thing itself; it is, further, the resistance which in each case invariably displayed this subjugation, the Protean wriggles by way of defence and reaction, and further, the results of successful counter-efforts. . . . What I mean is this: even partial loss of *utility*, decay, and degeneration, loss of function and purpose, in a word, death, appertain to the condition of the genuine *progressus*; which always appears in the shape of a will and a way to *greater* power, and is always realized at the expense of innumerable smaller powers. The magnitude of a 'progressus' is gauged by the greatness of the sacrifice that it requires: humanity as a mass sacrificed at the expense of the prosperity of the one *stronger* species of Man—that would be progress.[43]

At least, this makes it obvious that all active force in the world is of the nature of the Will to Power. This is a sort of life-force which is the Nietzchean will and it basically resembles Schopenhauer's will, with the exception that, whereas Schopenhauer is pessimistic about the final outcome, Nietzsche thinks it possible that things will turn out for the best.

Josiah Royce seems to me to be the American philosopher who has most nearly approximated a metaphysics of will. This is a point of interpretation which has been somewhat neglected by students of his thought.[44] Will is what is effective in the order of thought. Since Royce was an absolute idealist, it could be argued that he was also an absolute voluntarist. In

The World and the Individual, Royce defined will as the conscious fulfillment of purpose.

By will I mean here not any abstract psychological power or principle so to be named. I speak here of will not as of any causally efficacious entity whatever. I refer only to the mere fact of any one's consciousness, insisted upon in these discussions from the start, namely, the fact that the contents of an idea are present to mind as the actual embodiment and relative fulfillment of a present purpose, such as for instance you find embodied when you count or sing.[45]

Royce formally aligned himself with voluntarism, in an essay published in 1911, and recognized pragmatism or instrumentalism as belonging in the same category. But he rejected the relativistic version of voluntarism and insisted that will, "defines the truth that it endlessly seeks as a truth that possesses completeness, totality, self-possession, and therefore absoluteness."[46] Oddly enough, he added that will finds its freest expression in the mathematical sciences.[47]

Since he considered that the work of the philosopher was to discover what experience is and means,[48] Royce related willing very closely with knowing. "Every idea," he noted, "is as much a volitional process as it is an intellectual process."[49] Purposiveness is basic to volition, to cognition, and indeed, to being. Royce maintained:

To be means simply to express, to embody the complete internal meaning of a certain absolute system of ideas,—a system, moreover, which is genuinely implied in the true internal meaning or purpose of every finite idea, however fragmentary.[50]

His purpose, as a philosopher, is to express experience in a series of propositions that are mutually consistent; these ideal

propositions would be such that to deny them would be to re-
affirm them.[51] So, for Royce, willing implies the mental initiative required to alter the facts of experience, over and above
the manner in which they are passively received by intellect.[52]

At least four acts of willing are distinguished by Royce:
desire, choice, volitional expression, and attention. Desire
names the initial feelings that arise in the mind, which feelings
may be rational or irrational. All more developed acts of volition begin as desires.[53] Choice is a more rational process, involving "the presence of plans for the satisfaction of desires."
In choice, some desires are consciously made to survive and
this involves the suppression of other feelings.[54] Volitional
expression designates the effectiveness of willing; as Royce
puts it: "as doer, as voluntary agent, he [man] is the source
of new being; he is an originator."[55] Finally, there is the act
of attention, which is central to all volition. One attends, "by
dwelling upon one or another various already known and
abstractly conceivable possibilities."[56] Attention is the generic
act of volition, present to some extent in all other acts of
willing.

We are responsible for the consequences, to ourselves and
to other persons, of actions which we perform with attention.[57] Royce's analysis of willing is used in the practical
order, both in his ethics and his political philosophy.[58] Obviously, the ethics of loyalty implies the development of reasonable foresight, so that one may choose the action whose
consequences, "form the most satisfactory present experience
that is possible."[59]

It may be observed, in conclusion, that Royce has a very
suggestive and well-developed theory of volition. His views
have had a wide influence, not only in the United States and
Latin America but also in contemporary France. Men like
Gabriel Marcel, Louis Lavelle and Paul Ricoeur are not far

removed from Royce's basic notions of volition.[60] When Marcel writes that, "the will is embodied in acts which themselves form part of what I call reality," and that, "the will appears as a resistance to the seductions to which desire exposes me," he is not only thinking with Royce but using his very terminology.[61]

What we have seen, in this chapter, is the continuity of a tradition which makes reality to be ultimately of the nature of volition. Some thinkers identify this metaphysical will with the divine will; others make it personal volition; still others see it as a universal or cosmic will. Usually, such voluntaristic metaphysics results in an extension of the meaning of will to the point where it becomes as broad as being itself. This is a philosophical meaning that is far removed from the usage of ordinary language.

NOTES

1. Plotinus, *Enneads*, VI, 8, 1–21, ed. Bréhier, tome VI, deuxième partie, pp. 132–161.

2. Cf. Aristotle, *Nicomachean Ethics*, III, 1, 1109b28-1111b3.

3. *Enneads*, VI, 8, 1; ed. Bréhier, p. 134, line 31, for *boulesis*, and sect. 13, p. 150, line 27, for *thelesis*.

4. *Ibid.*, sect. 21; ed. Bréhier, p. 160.

5. E. Benz, *Marius Victorinus und die Entwicklung der abendländischen Willensmetaphysik* (Stuttgart, 1932). Benz thinks that Aristotle considered the will to be a special potency of the rational soul (p. 12, note 10) and regards Aristotelian psychology as the beginning of a will metaphysics.

6. M. Victorinus, *Liber de generatione divina*, 23 (PL VIII, 1031–1032); see the analysis in Gilson, *History of Christian Philosophy*, p. 588.

7. Cf. L. Gardet et M.-M. Anawati, *Introduction à la théologie musulmane* (Paris: Vrin, 1948), pp. 52–66, for the views of Al Ash'ari.

8. Avicebron, *Fons Vitae ex Arabico in Latinum translatus,* V, 38; ed. Cl. Baeumker, *BGPM,* I (Münster, 1892–1895), p. 326.

9. *Ibid.,* V, 38; p. 327.

10. *Ibid.,* V, 17; p. 289.

11. S. Munk, *Mélanges de philosophie juive et arabe* (Paris, 1859); reprinted, Paris: Vrin, 1927.

12. *Ibid.,* p. 101, note 3.

13. *Ibid.,* pp. 248–259.

14. For a summary of these textual problems and of A. Borisov's Russian study ("On the Point of Departure of the Voluntarist Philosophy of Solomon Ibn Gabirol," in *Bulletin of the USSR Academy of Social Sciences,* 1933), see: George Vajda's review in *Revue des Etudes Juives,* 98 (1934), 100–103. This journal was made available through the courtesy of the University of Minnesota Library.

15. Cf. J. Guttmann, *Die Philosophie des Salomon Ibn Gabirol* (Göttingen, 1889), pp. 265–266; and the thesis, Majer Bieler, *Der göttliche Wille (Logosbegriff) bei Gabirol* (Würzburg University, 1933).

16. See Gilson, *History of Christian Philosophy,* p. 649 (on Avicebron); p. 666 (the influence on Thomas of York); and p. 672 (for Albert's borrowings).

17. N. Malebranche, *De la recherche de la vérité,* VI, 2, 3; ed. G. Lewis, 3 vols. (Paris: Vrin, 1945), II, 200.

18. *Entretiens sur la métaphysique et sur la religion,* VII; in the trans. by M. Ginsberg (London: Allen and Unwin, 1925), p.189.

19. *Ibid.,* p. 191.

20. *Ibid.,* p. 196.

21. *Ibid.,* pp. 194–195.

22. A. Geulincx, *Ethica;* see the selection translated in Leibniz, *The Monadology,* by R. Latta (London: Oxford University Press, 1925), p. 330.

23. Schelling, *System des transcendentalen Idealismus* (Tübingen, 1800); the quotation is from a selection translated in the *Journal of Speculative Philosophy,* I (1867), 159–165.

24. F. Thilly, *History of Philosophy* (New York: Holt, 1931), p. 451; note that this quotation is not from the revised edition.

25. J. G. Fichte, *The Vocation of Man,* ed. R. Chisolm, p. 118, *op. cit.*

26. *Ibid.,* p. 28.

27. W. E. Hocking, *Types of Philosophy,* 3rd ed. (New York: Scribner, 1959), p. 186.

28. *The Vocation of Man,* ed. Chisolm, p. 124.

29. G. W. F. Hegel, *Rechtsphilosophie,* (1821); the English is from *The Ethics of Hegel,* trans. J. M. Sterrett (Boston: Ginn, 1893), pp. 116–117.

30. Hegel, *Philosophy of History,* trans. Sibree, p. 38.

31. R. Taylor, "Introduction," to: *The Will to Live: Selected Writings of A. Schopenhauer* (New York: Doubleday Anchor Books, 1962), pp. xi–xii.

32. *The Essays of Arthur Schopenhauer,* trans. T. Bailey Saunders (New York: Willey Book Co.), n.d., II, 591.

33. *Ueber den Willen in der Natur,* in *Sämtliche Werke,* ed. A. Hübscher (Wiesbaden: Brockhaus, 1950), Bd. IV. For a similar historical survey by Schopenhauer, see *Parerga und Paralipomena, Werke,* 1946, Bd. V, pp. 143 ff.

34. The first essay in *Die beiden Grundprobleme der Ethik* (*Werke,* Bd. IV, pp. 3–102) is the *Preisschrift* (1839) which has been translated as *Essay on the Freedom of the Will,* ed. K. Kolenda (New York: Liberal Arts Press, 1960).

35. *The World as Will and Idea,* 3 vols., trans. R. B. Haldane and J. Kemp (London: Kegan Paul, 1907–1909).

36. *Ibid.,* p. 129.

37. *Ibid.,* p. 130.

38. *Ibid.,* p. 143.

39. E. von Hartmann, *Philosophy of the Unconscious,* trans. W. C. Coupland (London: Trübner, 1884), p. 70.

40. *Ibid.*

41. J. Collins, *History of Modern European Philosophy,* p. 799.

42. Cf. W. Kaufmann, *Nietzsche: Philosopher, Psychologist, Antichrist* (New York: Meridian Books, 1959), pp. 5–7; and N. H. Cassem, "The Way to Wisdom: A Biodoctrinal Study of Nietzsche," *The Modern Schoolman,* XXXIX (1962), 352.

43. *Zur Genealogie der Moral,* II, ch. 12; in *Complete Works of F. Nietzsche,* ed. O. Levy (Edinburgh-London: T. N. Foulis, 1910).

44. For an exception, see: S. M. Thompson, "Idealism and Voluntarism in Royce," *Review of Metaphysics,* IX (1956), 433–440.

45. J. Royce, *The World and the Individual* (written 1899) (New York: Dover, 1959), vol. I, 326.

46. "Essay IV: The Problem of Truth," in *William James and Other Essays* (New York: Macmillan, 1911), pp. 187–254; the quotation is from page 236.

47. *Ibid.,* p. 238.

48. *The World and the Individual,* p. xvii.

49. *Ibid.*, p. 311.

50. *Ibid.*, p. 36.

51. *Ibid.*, p. xvii.

52. *Ibid.*, pp. 436–439.

53. *The Conception of God* (New York: Macmillan, 1897), p. 187.

54. *Ibid.*, pp. 187–188.

55. *The World and the Individual*, p. 439.

56. *The Conception of God*, p. 192.

57. *Fugitive Essays* (Cambridge: Harvard University Press), 1920, p. 209.

58. See the whole Essay, "The Nature of Voluntary Progress," in *Fugitive Essays*, pp. 96–132.

59. "Tests of Right and Wrong," *Fugitive Essays*, p. 209.

60. For Lavelle, see: "Les trois moments de la métaphysique," in *L'Activité Philosophique*, ed. M. Farber (Paris: Presses Universitaires, 1950), vol. II, 132–148; and R. Lazzarini, "Intentionalism and Contemporary Currents of Spiritualist Philosophy," *International Philosophical Quarterly*, I (1961), 324. For Ricoeur, see his *Philosophie de la volonté* (Paris: Aubier, 1949).

61. See G. Marcel, *The Mystery of Being* (Chicago: Regnery, 1951), p. 110.

A Core Meaning of Will

CHAPTER X

A Core Meaning of Will

THIS FINAL CHAPTER is devoted to an examination of psychological investigations of the volitional processes and to an attempt to conclude to a philosophically useful definition of will.

In 1929, the Court of Appeals of the District of Columbia stated the following norm to be applied in criminal cases in which the defendant attempts an insanity defense:

The accepted rule in this day and age . . . is that the accused must be capable, not only of distinguishing between right and wrong, but that he was not impelled to do the act by an ir-resistible impulse, which means before it will justify a verdict of acquittal that his reasoning powers were so far dethroned by his diseased mental condition as to deprive him of the will power to resist the insane impulse to perpetrate the deed, though know-ing it to be wrong.[1]

Implied in the statement of this legal rule is a certain practical view of human volition and its surrounding mental functions which seems to me to be basic to Western thought. I do not say that the Court has clearly defined its terms; most certainly, it has not done that. Instead, it relied on the assumption that most educated people in twentieth-century America would know the meaning of words like impulse, reasoning powers and will power.

One might expect some clarification of what it means to will, from psychology. As a discipline distinct from philosophy, scientific psychology is now roughly one hundred years old. It began in mid-nineteenth century with the efforts of German scholars at Leipzig and Würzburg to study man's conscious activities in an experimental manner. Men like E. H. Weber, Gustav Fechner and Wilhelm Wundt approached the investigation of human behavior, using some of the techniques of physiology and with the philosophical preconceptions of Kant and Herbart. Wundt is usually regarded as the "father" of experimental psychology because he established the first specialized laboratory for psychology, at Leipzig.[2] He was interested in volitional functions but he reacted against the notion that the will is a faculty of the human soul and he concentrated on introspective studies of feelings, impulses, desires and choices.[3] For Wundt, will in the individual man is not an elementary process but a construction elaborated out of a complex of various basic impulses and feelings.[4] The introspective technique provided Wundt with what he regarded as factual data (the personal reports by his subjects on their own conscious experiences while performing certain tasks) which he interpreted by means of the philosophical principle of sufficient reason. Thus, for Wundt, will came to mean that unification and organization of experienced impulses and feelings which would seem to account for what is ordinarily called volitional activity.

Oswald Külpe initiated the use of the introspective method at Würzburg. His pupil, Narziss Ach, applied this technique to the study of volitional experience.[5] Ach criticized Wundt's conclusion (that no will-act, as such, was experimentally discoverable) and maintained that the mechanical character of the tasks performed by the subjects in the Wundtian laboratory precluded properly volitional activity. Ach also insisted that Wundt's investigations had failed to concentrate on the period *prior* to the performance of a task. It was felt at Würzburg that willing might be more evident in the subjects' advance acceptance of the task than in the actual execution of it.

Ach endeavored to treat introspective evidence in a more systematic, or rigorously scientific, manner. He distinguished the "determining tendency" as the way in which the assigned task was brought to termination; he also focussed attention on *Bewusstheit*, that is, the content of consciousness which is neither image nor sensation.[6] In practice, Ach took a group of persons, presented them with nonsense syllables (e.g. "funip"), directed them to choose one of several possible tasks (e.g. to interchange the first and third letters, to substitute for the first consonant the next consonant in the alphabet, and so on). At first, Ach found little evidence of any determining tendency ("I will" do this). He proceeded to make the tasks more difficult, had his subjects first memorize pairs of nonsense words, then instructed them to overcome this acquired association or reproductive tendency by performing a task that was different from simple reproduction. The preliminary learning plus the changing of the task provided an "obstacle" which was calculated to require effort for its resolution. The subjects were asked to make detailed reports on their conscious feelings during the period of such effort. Physiological devices were also used to record bodily changes associated with the experience of performing these tasks.

Ultimately, Ach described four aspects of the responses of his subjects: a) a *sensorial* element, involving muscular tension, feelings of strain and kinesthetic sensations; b) a *dynamic* element, in which the subject becomes aware of effort; c) an *intellectual* element, in which the end and means to attain it are known; and d) a *consciousness of resolving*, where there is an immediate awareness of *self* as the ultimate source initiating the determining tendency.[7]

Particularly in reference to item d), Ach claimed to have isolated, as a basic datum, a moment in consciousness which is irreducible and is an instance of "I will." Note that this finding by Ach is directly contradictory to the view of Wundt. Some present-day psychologists regard this presumed isolation of the will-function as Ach's most significant contribution.[8] It is not our task to comment on the scientific character of Ach's results but simply to suggest what view of will they imply. Ach eventually took will to mean some sort of personal effort to resolve a problem. This resolution was taken to be an activity of the self. He decided that the subject, in willing, adopts a certain goal of activity and endeavors to persevere in this activity until its terminaton. Thus described, will names a process of auto-determination on the conscious level.

At Louvain University (Belgium) during the early part of this century, similar studies were carried on in the psychology laboratory directed by Albert Michotte. He and his many students had some training in Scholastic philosophy and they tended to identify willing with choosing. Where Ach's experiments had followed the pattern, "I will do X when Y appears," the Louvain experiments took the form, "I will do X or Z when Y appears." Emphasis was thus placed on the choice between X or Z.[9] In one series of experiments at Louvain, the subjects were presented with two numbers concerning which they were to make a choice: to add or subtract for the smaller numbers, to multiply or divide for the larger ones. The subjects had previously learned to associate addition with the smaller and multiplication with the larger. In this way the Louvain investigators retained from Ach the technique of the obstacle, while adding the new feature of an alternative which provided for choice. The subjects pressed a key to indicate their choices but were not required to carry the task to completion. Immediately on making the choice, they were asked to make introspective reports of their experiences. From such data, Michotte concluded that, besides the various psychic functions of sensation, cognition and feeling, the act of choosing involves some irreducible center of activity.[10] In other words, Michotte considered that he had evidence of a distinctive will-function.

Other psychologists trained at Louvain pushed these studies into somewhat new areas. Boyd Barrett accepted the findings of Michotte in regard to choosing but investigated the experiences involved in *completing* tasks. Motivation eventually became a central concept in Boyd Barrett's writing.[11] His subjects included professors and advanced students at Louvain University. They provided introspective data concerning the choosing and drinking of various colorless liquids which were ranked according to agreeableness. Boyd Barrett does not claim that his studies revealed a direct awareness of "will power" but his interpretation tends to support the traditional meaning of will which is common in textbooks of Scholastic rational psychology. He seems to have been convinced that the human will is a spiritual faculty whose *activity* is open to introspection, that volition is irreducible to lower impulses and feelings, and that various degrees of strength are distinguishable among acts of willing.[12] How close he came to the position of traditional Scholasticism may be judged from the following description.

Many words and phrases denote volitional activities. 'To make up one's mind,' to resolve, to consent, to desire, to strive, to choose, to make an effort—these infinitives point to will acts. Conation, intention, willing, inhibiting, controlling, permitting, preventing, and many such words are also used of the will. When a man of character, at some crisis of his life, *makes up his mind* to adopt a certain course, and says, 'I will do so and so. I am determined to do it. It is my firm intention to do it'—he is speaking of a certain state of soul that we call *willing*. This state is radically different from all other states. It is about action. It is emotional. It concerns self and is very personal. It is creative and arbitrary. It means self determination. Self rules self. It is about the future. It is about reality. It is something almost sacred.[13]

Boyd Barrett claimed that his findings were "simply and purely empirical," particularly with regard to an equation purporting to give the psychological character of a given person.[14] In these equations a certain amount of will power was included, along with other psychic factors. In effect, Boyd Barrett adopted a personalistic view of will, as a higher faculty of the human soul.

In the United States of America, in 1920, a direct rebuttal to the findings of the Ach-Michotte-Barrett group was entered by R. H. Wheeler.[15] His interpretation reflects the philosophical commitment of naturalism. Wheeler conducted experiments similar to the European ones (the American subjects made selections from various photographs) and he assembled retrospective reports from his subjects. Contrary to the conclusions of Würzburg and Louvain, Wheeler claimed that his subjects reported no unanalyzable experience of "willing." Their conscious experiences in choosing reduced to various organic, sensory and kinesthetic processes.[16] In other words, Wheeler denied the empirical validity of the personalistic, spiritual-minded, faculty-theory interpretation of human volition.

An American personalistic psychologist, Mary Whiton

Calkins, then entered the lists in opposition to Wheeler's stand.[17] Miss Calkins bluntly accused Wheeler of ignoring the obvious meaning of certain terms in his subjects' reports ("I must," and "I find myself") which to her mind testified to a rather direct awareness of will as self-activity. Repeating some of Wheeler's experiments, she found further evidence which she interpreted as revealing an irreducible element ("I will") in acts of choosing. Such diversity in interpretation suggests that philosophical preconceptions continued to influence the psychological interpretation of laboratory reports on the experiences associated with choice.

Also during the 1920's, at the University of London, Francis Aveling directed studies of volition, using modifications of the Louvain techniques. These British investigations included the use of various mechanical devices (chiefly the psycho-galvanometer and the pneumograph) to record physiological responses connected with willing. In general, Aveling found evidence of *effort* preceding and following the moment of decision but he noticed little physical modification at the time of resolution. Hence he concluded that strong feelings of effort were lacking at the moment of actual resolve. He attributed the critical act of willing to the self and described the moment of decision as an adoption of "the motive or motives for the selection of one of the alternatives."[18] Aveling shares a rather widespread tendency in Europe to shift from the language of volition into that of motivation.

Among the pupils of Aveling, Raphael McCarthy tried to make quantitative measurements of "conation"—what he seems to have regarded as the inclining force of will. On this matter his results were negative: he found it impossible to apply quantitative methods to the measuring of will power.[19] McCarthy's research tended to confirm Ach's findings, to the effect that some sort of effort at resolution of a conflict of alternatives is central to volition. However, McCarthy placed more emphasis on *attention*, in this process of volitional resolution, than Ach had done.[20]

Honoria M. Wells, another pupil of Aveling, undertook to make a thorough description of "all the processes occurring during an act of voluntary choice."[21] Her approach clearly owes something to the philosophical method of phenomenology. In experiments similar to those of Boyd Barrett, Miss Wells employed physiological techniques as well as introspective reports. She concluded that there is observable evidence of direct awareness of personal willing. Her position is like that of Miss Calkins, for Miss Wells knew and criticized the non-personalistic views of Wheeler. The following excerpt indicates the nature of Miss Well's conclusions.

We hold that a direct awareness of the 'self' (the logical subject of experience) is to be found among the processes constituting the total volitional consciousness. . . . In this awareness, therefore, we have a unique experience in which the 'self' as subject cognizes itself, and itself as acting.[22]

A great deal of psychological literature concerning the processes of volition has appeared in Germany during the past eighty years. We have already noted something of the views of the first German psychologists, up to the work of Ach. The German interest in the subject continued unabated, through the first three decades of this century. Most of this activity has been well digested in a book published by Werner Haensel in 1939.[23] He covers the studies of the following psychologists and philosophers: Ebbinghaus, Wundt, Münsterberg, Meumann, Lipps, Pfänder, Wentscher, Ach, Lindworsky, Hönigswald, Scheler, von Hildebrand,

Edith Stein, Reiner and Volkelt.[24] Haensel's own thesis is that willing is a process identical with that of *motivation*.[25] Many of the thinkers that he studied do move in that direction, to assert that a man's choices and decisions are somewhat dictated by the values and ideals to which they attend.

This trend in German psychology is well illustrated by the work of J. Lindworsky. He established his laboratory at Cologne and his major work was published in 1923.[26] Of course, Lindworksy knew the work of Ach and Michotte and he was also familiar with the American controversy between Miss Calkins and Wheeler. Repeating experiments similar to those done at Würzburg, Lindworksy disagreed in part with Ach's interpretation of basically the same data. He admitted that Ach had been right on two points: (1) the course of a volitional action does depend on the acceptance of a task; and (2) there is a "determining tendency" which does not reduce to mere impulses and feelings.[27] However, Lindworsky denied that the force of the determining tendency (in other words, will power) depends on the vigor of the resolve to perform the task. He claimed that some subjects start with a resolution to carry out the task but make no effort, later, to recall such a resolution. Other subjects, according to Lindworsky, do strive to keep their resolve in the forefront of consciousness. Those in the first group were, in effect, judged by Ach to be weak-willed, when in fact they were simply inattentive. So, *attention* came to be stressed by Lindworsky as a key element in the volitional process. "Will power" is equated with "consciousness of resolve." As Lindworsky puts it, "our will appears to be comparable not to a forceful stroke of a hammer, but, rather, to a switching, or a closing of a contact, for which no particular force is necessary."[28]

Instead of volitional accomplishment being dependent on strength of will, it varies directly with the availability of motives to which the subject continues to attend. Thus Lindworsky is typical of a general tendency in the German psychological writings to shift the focal point of volition from the concept of will-as-force, with varying degrees of intensity, toward an emphasis on attentive awareness of certain ideals or *values* which function in motivating the apparently strong-willed person. As Lindworsky sums up his position:

It is of little or no importance for the execution of a resolution whether or not the resolution has been made very energetically and intensely. On the other hand, it is of the greatest importance that the resolution be in consciousness at the very moment when it is to be carried out; if this is the case, its execution is certain, provided, of course, that it is still a genuine resolution and an actual decision.[29]

There is patent common sense in many of Lindworsky's findings. He has doubtless offered a possible explanation of phenomena of the present day: brain washing, the practical utility of repeated propaganda, and even the effects of reiterated advertising claims.

From the 1930's onward, the United States became the country in which empirical psychologists were most active and influential. However, the interests of recent American psychologists have not been directed to studies of volition. The term "will" is rarely found in the literature of present-day American psychology. During the past fifteen years, for instance, *Psychological Abstracts* reports practically no American studies of will or volition, as such. This is not to say that the subject is entirely ignored; rather, researchers have shifted to a different terminology, decision-making, motivation, evaluation, and so on. As Norman Munn explains the situation, writing in 1951:

While they have much popular usage, the terms *will* and *will power* are seldom used by psychologists because they really explain nothing. . . . Psychologists have come to regard the varieties of behavior attributed to 'will power' as expressions of the relative strength of motive.[30]

In a more recent textbook by a group of American psychologists, this exclusion of the language of volition is spelled out in greater detail.

Although psychologists must depart somewhat from observation—because observations alone never interpret themselves—they still stay as close to observation as is practicable. In an earlier age, there was a tendency to explain things in terms of concepts called 'essences,' that the thinker devised or found ready-made in his society. Thus a great deal was said about things like 'mind' or 'will' or 'conscience,' all of which were used as explanatory terms. Today we are wary of using these terms, simply because they get a long way from the actual observations themselves. . . . It is difficult, if not impossible, to observe a will or a mind or a conscience. . . . Therefore, according to the law of parsimony, we should drop our 'will chooses' etc. and just say 'I choose.'[31]

One may remark in passing on the naiveté of writers who appear to consider "I" a simpler or more observable item than "will." However, the main point is clear: recent psychological literature offers little help in the understanding of the language of volition, precisely because will is excluded as non-explanatory and non-scientific. Meanwhile, will continues to be used in popular and scholarly writings, in spite of the ban that experimental psychologists have put upon it.

Ironically, we find a reverse trend in clinical psychology, psychoanalysis and psychiatry. Sigmund Freud had no technical use for the language of willing. His basic terminology of the id, ego and super-ego enabled him to talk about human behavior without mentioning volition.[32] This was precisely one of the criticisms directed against the original Freudianism by some of Freud's disciples. Alfred Adler (at one time, Freud's secretary) broke with the master in 1911 and went on to establish the school of "Individual Psychology."[33] One of Adler's chief complaints against Freud was that the libido (unconscious sexual drives) was made the source of the energy in man's psychic life. Adler came to insist that "will to power" (*Wille zur Macht*), in a modified Nietzschean sense, was much more important than Freud had realized. One of Adler's pupils, Rudolph Allers, developed the theme of two primitive tendencies of human nature, the will to power and the will to community.[34] The first is a tendency toward preservation of the self; the second is directed toward the social good. In this view, will is a primal tendency of man's nature.

Another pupil of Freud, Otto Rank, departed from the original theory and made "will therapy" the basis of his treatment of psychic disorders. Rank claimed that Freud had reduced willing to the activity of the *Id*, while Adler had interpreted will sociologically, as the will to power.[35] What is advisable in the treatment of emotional disorders, Rank insisted, is to encourage him to assert his "positive will."[36] At no point in his book on will therapy does Rank say precisely what this will is. The general impression one gets is that the Rankian concept of will covers the conscious personal ability to make an effort, to wish and to strive for control of various impulses, for the sake of certain ideal values. In a recent summary of Rank's view, we find the following description.

[Will is] a positive guiding organization and integration of self which creatively utilizes as well as inhibits and controls the instinctive drives. When it is added . . . we have not only motive force but direction as well. The will . . . is a generalized impulse toward integrated affective expression which is prior to growth and development and which determines what the integrated personality will be.[37]

One American school in which Rank has had some influence is the non-directive therapy of Carl Rogers and his associates. While Roger's program as a clinical psychology has the emphasis on self-realization which distinguishes the Rankian approach, the language of will is not central in non-directive therapy.[38] However, one of Roger's pupils, Charles A. Curran, has applied the theory to religious counselling, making some use of a modern Thomistic terminology of psychic faculties, in which will is rational appetite.[39]

Other occasional and sporadic suggestions are found in the literature of clinical psychology, psychoanalysis and psychiatry to the effect that personal will-effort may have some utility in treating emotional and mental disorders. Practical psychology continues, then, to make some use of the term "will" but it is difficult to discern any definite meaning of the term in these studies.[40]

Soviet psychologists seem to take a very simple and rather sensible view of human will. The subject is treated in their works on educational psychology.[41] They speak of will power as an indispensable factor in man's psychic life. As they see it, the general feature of willing is effort to overcome obstacles. Volition involves setting up a conscious aim and working toward this goal by purposive activity.[42] The Polish scholar, Józef Reutt, reports as follows in an article published in 1952:

The question of the definition of will is not given the same uniform and indisputable character as accorded to the general characteristic of volitional processes. The definitions of will put forward by Soviet scientists are not quite alike in their meaning. In one instance, an act of will is called the conscious and intentional activity of man which tends to reach a definite end (Kairow), and in another, all specifically human actions are termed as acts of will (Rubinstein). It is also said of will that it is a system of movements linked together by a common aim and one sole motive (Kornilow) and that it is that part of psychic life which manifests itself in consciously directing actions towards certain ends.[43]

One may note the stress, in Russian psychology, on the end-directed character of volitional activity. As would be expected, ends are considered appropriate when they are in keeping with the welfare of society and the state. It is quite clear that the training of the will of the child is an important part of the educational program in the Soviet Union. Hard work and a severe way of life are regarded as essential to the development of a strong will.[44]

In summary appraisal of what psychologists have to say about will, one is forced to conclude that the results, particularly in the experimental field, are of little value to our present investigation. In the early period of experimental studies, from Ach to Lindworsky, it is evident that philosophical assumptions are operative in the various and conflicting interpretations offered for much the same introspective data. Some psychologists have maintained that what amounts to a faculty of will is well grounded in their scientific observations; other psychologists have been equally sure that there is no experimental evidence of will-functions which cannot be reduced to initial impulses and feelings of a somewhat physiological character. As we have seen, many experimental psychologists now regard will as a non-scientific term. Some continued interest in volition has been noted among applied psychologists, psychoanalysts and psychiatrists. Here, the meaning given to will is personal effort toward self-actualization and integration.

In view of the negative findings in psychology, we may well ask, now, whether the language of volition has any basic significance for those who engage in serious study of human activities. However, I think that there is an established core-meaning for will. This signification is not only that which is loosely described in general dictionaries but also that which is analyzed and expressed under diverse terminologies in several of the main schools of philosophy.

As I see it, this central meaning of human willing may be found in philosophies as diverse as the thought of Thomas Aquinas, Josiah Royce, John Dewey and the Soviet psychologists. Obviously, these thinkers represent radically different types of thought and terminology—yet each school offers something useful to our core-meaning.

Aquinas talks about at least five distinct acts of willing: intention of an end, consent to means, choice of a means (or, of action or non-action), volitional use of other activities, and volitional enjoyment of what has been accomplished through volition. He also discusses but less clearly: the act of wishing an end (*velle*), the act of desiring (*desiderium*), and the act of loving. The relating of these last three to the initial five volitional functions is a difficult problem.

Josiah Royce described four acts of willing: desiring,

attending, choosing and effectuating one's choices or decisions. In Royce's analysis, all will actions following upon initial desires or feelings are acts of attention. A person attends by concentrating on one desire while suppressing others, and by relating choice and effectuation to some governing ideal to which attention is directed.

John Dewey's instrumentalist description provides us with four stages of volition: the feeling of impulses, the effort to reflect on consequences, the decision to act or refrain from acting, and the voluntary execution of the action. He may even have a fifth step: the feeling of reflective satisfaction in the success, or social value, of accomplished activity.

Soviet educational psychology distinguishes at least five stages in the activity of willing, each of which requires what is plainly called personal effort: fixing upon a certain goal of activity, endeavoring to overcome obstacles to this aim, choosing, resolving (in the sense of definitely "making up one's mind to act"), and the execution of one's resolution in either, a) external process (bodily activity), or b) internal process (a psychic effort to refrain from acting). Russian psychologists also speak of spontaneous impulses in the child, and of the need for their voluntary control. In addition, they continually stress the value of willing to concentrate on social ideals.

Now none of these analyses necessarily implies that every complete volitional process must go through all the stages described, or in the order in which they are named, or with a full awareness of the performance of each step. Habit formation is a phenomenon recognized in all four of the key philosophies under consideration. The psychic effect of habituation is to fuse abstractly distinguished steps into one smooth act of willing which becomes easier and requires less forceful attention on the part of the mature agent.

As William James put it, in the language of physiology, habit formation is like the wearing of a groove in the channel of ideo-motor discharge: the result is a smoother flow of will energy.[45]

If we overlook the obvious variations of terminology in these analyses, we find something that looks like a common pattern. *Step I* consists of certain unresolved, initial feeling-tendencies or impulses. *Step II* is the initiation of the personal effort to resolve the conflict of these impulses in terms of some reflective objective (which may be called an end, a conscious purpose, or an ideal value). *Step III* is the conscious terminating of the resolving process, in decision or choice. *Step IV* is the controlled execution of the decision, in volitionally directed activity or omission of activity. *Step V* is reflective satisfaction (or dissatisfaction) with the consequences of such a process.

One could define the central meaning of willing by saying that it is what is involved in the accomplishment of the foregoing five steps in personal effort making. Equivalent definitions could be contrived by using the notions of *personal effort, appetition, freedom,* or *love* as generic features. The following descriptive definition is what I would propose, at the end of much reading on the subject. *Willing is that psychic activity of man, whereby he tends toward or away from certain objectives reflectively adopted, whereby he sometimes achieves personal freedom of action, whereby he acts with some spontaneity or self-initiative, and whereby he approves or loves what he deems good and disapproves or hates what he deems not good.*

It should be added that such a meaning for volition need not commit the user to any special view of will as a power or faculty. Nor should it be understood as excluding rational motivation. Our core-definition does not tell us all about volition. No mere definition can do that. Our statement of what willing means is adequate, if it enables philosophers and other serious students of human activities to discuss volition with some mutual understanding.

NOTES

1. Smith v. United States, 59 App. D.C. 144, 145, 36 F. 2d, 548, 549 (1929); cited and discussed in C. W. Halleck, "The Insanity Defense in the District of Columbia—A Legal Lorelei," *Georgetown Law Journal*, 49 (1960), 296.

2. See E. G. Boring, *A History of Experimental Psychology* (New York: Appleton-Century-Crofts, 1950), pp. 323–339.

3. "It is in the doctrine of feeling and will more than anywhere else that psychology still wears the fetters of the old faculty theory. . . . We must pronounce this theory a purely imaginary construction from beginning to end. It has taken its facts from every possible source except an unprejudiced introspection." W. Wundt, *Human and Animal Psychology*, translated from the German edition (1896) by J. E. Creighton and E. B. Titchener (New York: Macmillan, 1901), pp. 224–225.

4. Wundt has, of course, a great deal to say about "will" and he is sometimes classified as a philosophical voluntarist. In the work cited above, *Lecture* 15 (pp. 223–234) treats the relation of feeling to willing, impulse and desire, development of will, simple and complex voluntary acts, psychological elements in voluntary actions. *Lecture* 29 (pp. 423–436) deals with voluntary action, causality of the will, relation of the individual to the general will, character of the ultimate cause of will.

5. N. Ach, *Ueber den Willensakt und das Denken* (Göttingen: Vandenhoech und Ruprecht, 1905); *Ueber den Willensakt und das Temperament* (Leipzig: Quelle und Meyer, 1910); *Analyse des Wollens* (Berlin: Urban und Schwarzenberg, 1935); cf. O. Selz, "Die experimentelle Untersuchung des Willensaktes," *Zeitschrift für Psychologie*, 57 (1910), 241–270.

6. Cf. Boring, *op. cit.*, pp. 405–406.

7. This summary is taken from T. V. Moore, *The Driving Forces*

of *Human Nature and their Adjustment* (New York: Greene and Stratton, 1948), p. 321; based on Ach, *Analyse des Wollens*, pp. 415 ff.

8. See M. B. Arnold and J. A. Gasson, *The Human Person* (New York: Ronald Press, 1954), p. 16; T. J. Gannon, *Psychology: The Unity of Human Behavior* (New York: Ginn, 1945), p. 400.

9. A. Michotte et E. Prüm, "Etude expérimentale sur le choix volontaire et ses antécédents immédiats," *Archives de Psychologie*, X (1910–1911), 113–320.

10. For a description in English of the Louvain procedure and findings, see E. Boyd Barrett, *Motive-Force and Motivation-Tracks* (London: Longmans, Green, 1911), pp. 37–38.

11. See the book cited in note 10.

12. In a later book (*Strength of Will*, New York: P. J. Kenedy, 1915, p. 39), Boyd Barrett remarks: "We know little about the will. We are aware of its spiritual nature, and we can trace it roughly in some of its activities. We are familiar with some of the phenomena which accompany willing, but that is all. . . . We are conscious that willing is not thinking nor imagining. Most of us know little more."

13. *Strength of Will*, p. 41.

14. See the last chapter of his *Motivation-Force*, and especially p. 213, for the words just quoted.

15. Wheeler's main work is: *An Experimental Investigation of the Process of Choosing* (Eugene, Oregon: University of Oregon Publication, 1920).

16. For a summary of Wheeler's views, see H. G. Wyatt, *The Psychology of Intelligence and Will* (New York: Harcourt, Brace, 1931), pp. 234–235. Wyatt's own views on willing are generally similar to the position of John Dewey.

17. M. W. Calkins, "Fact and Inference in Raymond Wheeler's Doctrine of Will and Self-Activity," *Psychological Review*, XXVIII (1921), 356–374. She had stated her personalistic position some years earlier: "The Self and Scientific Psychology," *American Journal of Psychology*, XXVI (1915), 495–524.

18. F. Aveling, "St. Thomas and Modern Thought," in *St. Thomas Aquinas*, ed. C. Lattey (Cambridge, England: Heffer, 1925), p. 126. See also his "Emotion, Conation and Will," in *Feelings and Emotions*, ed. C. Murchison (Worcester: Clark University Press, 1928), p. 52. A more general summary of Aveling's later views is found in *Personality and Will* (New York: D. Appleton, 1931).

19. R. McCarthy, *The Measurement of Conation: An Enquiry*

into Volitional Processes (Chicago: Loyola University Press, 1926), pp. 6–7, 102–103.

20. *Ibid.*, p. 103.

21. H. M. Wells, "The Phenomenology of Acts of Choice," *British Journal of Psychology*, Monograph Supplement IV, 11 (1927), 1–155; the quotation is from the first page.

22. *Ibid.*, p. 140; see the whole of Chapter VI: "The Self as Phenomenon in Volitional Consciousness," pp. 130–145.

23. W. Haensel, *Beiträge zur Strukturanalyse des Wollens* (Leipzig: J. A. Barth, 1939).

24. *Ibid.*, pp. 8–82; in his bibliography, Haensel lists nearly all important German publications on will, for the past eighty years.

25. Haensel's concluding chapter (*ibid.*, pp. 83–160) is entitled: "Die Einheit von Motivation und Wollen."

26. J. Lindworsky, *Der Wille* (Leipzig: J. A. Barth, 1923). This work has not been translated but two of his more popular books are in English: *The Training of the Will*, translated by A. Steiner and E. A. Fitzpatrick (Milwaukee: Bruce, 1929); and *Experimental Psychology*, translated by H. A. De Silva (New York: Macmillan, 1931).

27. See *Experimental Psychology*, pp. 309–313; *Training of the Will*, pp. 35–37.

28. *Experimental Psyhology*, pp. 315–316.

29. *Ibid.*, p. 50.

30. N. L. Munn, *Psychology: The Fundamentals of Human Adjustment*, 2nd ed. (Boston: Houghton Mifflin, 1951), pp. 319–320.

31. Sartain, North, Strange and Chapman, *Psychology: Understanding Human Behavior* (New York: McGraw-Hill, 1958), p 331; in Prathro and Teska, *Psychology* (New York: Ginn, 1950), p. 368, will is dismissed as a "layman's term" for motive.

32. Cf. J. Nuttin, *Psychanalyse* (Louvain-Paris: Vrin, 1950), p. 216: "La Psychanalyse, de son coté, n'attribuait à la connaissance consciente qu'un rôle très secondaire . . . La psychologie du comportement et la psychologie profonde ont donc perdu de vue le processus de l'activité volontaire à but conscient et se situent à l'opposé de cette psychologie de la volonté."

33. A. Adler, *Praxis und Theorie der Individualpsychologie*, 3 Aufl. (München: Bergmann, 1927); *The Practice and Theory of Individual Psychology* (New York: Harcourt, Brace, 1927).

34. R. Allers, *Das Werden der sittlichen Person. Wesen und Erziehung des Charakters* (Freiburg i. B.: Herder, 1935); *The Psy-*

chology of Character (New York: Sheed and Ward, 1939), pp. 28–30, 75–86.

35. O. Rank, *Will Therapy and Truth and Reality* (New York: Knopf, 1950), pp. 10–11.

36. *Ibid.*, p. 19.

37. M. B. Arnold and J. A. Gasson, *The Human Person*, p. 159.

38. C. Rogers, *Client Centered Therapy* (Boston: Houghton Mifflin, 1951), pp. 478–497, for nineteen propositions which summarize his point of view.

39. C. A. Curran, *Counselling in Catholic Life and Education* (New York: Macmillan, 1952).

40. See for the past ten years: E. Forti, "Les dérèglements de la volonté et leur interprétation psychologique," *Egyptian Journal of Psychology*, VIII (1952), 117–138; P. Mullahy, "Will, Choice, and Ends," *Psychiatry*, XII (1949), 379–386; L. Lowrey, "Psychic Determinism and Responsibility," *Psychiatric Quarterly*, XXVII (1953), 543–562; E. M. Scott, "Will and Religion as Useful Adjuncts in Psychotherapy," *Psychical Reports*, I (1955), 379–381; A. Wheelis, "Will and Psychoanalysis," *Journal of the American Psychoanalytic Association*, IV (1956), 285–303.

41. Cf. K. I. Lebeden, "K Voprosu ob Izlozhenii Teorii Voli v Uchebnikakh Psikhologii," *Sovietskaya Pedagogia*, I (1950), 64–67.

42. J. Reutt, "Psychologia Woli w Nauce Radzieckien," *Przeglad Psychologiczny*, I (1952), 58–113; for an English summary, pp. 226–232.

43. *Ibid.*, p. 227.

44. *Ibid.*, pp. 231–232.

45. W. James, *Principles of Psychology*, 2 vols. (London: Macmillan, 1890), II, 526–527.

Index